Winning
Battles
With Love

Dr. C. V. White

Dr. C.V. White

Winning Battles with Love

Unless otherwise quoted all word definitions Greek and Hebrew and scripture quotations are from the King James Version of the Bible as recorded in the Blue Letter Bible: Retrieved from http://www.blueletterbible.org. All other scripture quotations from the amplified Bible were retrieved from the biblegateway.com by the Lockman Foundation or International Standard Bible

Encyclopedia, Electronic Database, Copyright © 1995-1996, 2003 by Biblesoft, Inc., All rights reserved, The New Unger's Bible Dictionary - Originally published by Moody Press of Chicago,Illinois, Copyright © 1988.

Published by:
Dr. C.V. White
formerly Fruit That Remains LLC
150 Post Office Road
Waldorf, Maryland 20604
Email: drcvwhite@gmail.com

ISBN 13: 978-1-934326-04-6
ISBN 10: 1-934326-04-6

DiViNE Purpose Publishing
www.divinepurposepublishing.com
P. O. Box 906
Branford, CT. 06405

Printed in the United States of America

DEDICATION

This book is dedicated to my biological father, Rev. Lee Andrew Townes Sr., who helped me to mature naturally and spiritually. He is the seed from which I came. My father was an inspiration to me as my father and as my pastor for many years. He started to preach when he was eight years old and continued for seventy-two years. For fifty of those years, he pastored churches. During that time, he was instrumental in the spiritual growth of many aspiring pastors and clergy.

Also, I thank Bishop Rodney S. Walker I, my spiritual father, who has been instrumental in my spiritual growth. Bishop Walker, I appreciate your support while I was attending school, working, and preparing for ministry. You have been and still are a great blessing to me! Every step of the way you encouraged me to continue with my writing projects. I am appreciative of all of your efforts to assist me in this project and in other areas of my life. I also appreciate God for giving me such a wonderful spiritual father in you! You are a special gift from God and I will always cherish everything that you have poured into me all of these years.

I want to thank my family every one is a blessing.

APPRECIATION

I would like to take this opportunity to thank Bishop Rodney S. Walker I, Paulette Walker, Lisa Burgess, Cynthia Anglin and Divine Purpose Publishing for their support and assistance in the preparation of this book for publication.

I appreciate your support and prayers that made it possible for me to complete the final preparation for printing and distribution of this book. Your ideas and suggestions contributed immensely to the success of this project. It was so good to have you as part of the team. I am confident that good things will come from our joint efforts. Thank you, again, for a job well done!

Table of Contents

Chapter 1 - The Origin of Love

First of all, the war is won but we as believer are going to have to fight some battles. If we want to succeed in winning any battle, we must begin with love. We must begin our conversations with love in mind. Operating in love is a lifestyle not just a state of mind. God began everything with love in mind. Love is the highest form of actions that God uses to get desired results. He saved the entire world with love. Love is a part of who God is and He does nothing without love in mine. God loved man before He created man; therefore His relationship with man is based on love. God's expectation is that man would receive His love and return His love. In addition God expects man to love himself and his fellow-man as God's creations. When the question was asked of Jesus what is the greatest commandment that you have given man His reply is found in Mathew 22:36-40.

Matthew 22:36-40

Master, which is the great commandment in the law? 37 Jesus said unto him, Thou shalt love the Lord thy God with all thy heart, and with all thy soul, and with all thy mind. 38 This is the first and great commandment. 39 And the second is like unto it, Thou shalt love thy neighbour as thyself. 40 On these two commandments hang all the law and the prophets.

Since this is the first and great commandment and all the law and the prophets hang on it, we must realize that we are not going to win anything without love. In other words, love is a partner to everything. As we explore this topic, we will see the different areas of love and how they are specific to different relationships but the bottom line is that the only way to win is with love.

As we begin to read the Old Testament, we will find God admonishing the people of God to love Him, because if they do that He can always win the battles they face. In addition, God is constantly reminding them that He loves them. It is easy to say you love someone but the proof is in the demonstration of His unconditional love. His love is the example that sets the tone and the understanding of what love really is. Many times people say that they love people, places or things but they have no understanding of what love really is. Love is not a feeling, it is a choice. God chose to love us without us having to do anything.

In order to understand what love really is, we must first identify the origin of love. One of the attributes of God is love and it is so important you cannot accomplish anything without exercising love nor can you win any battles without it. Notice what is said in 1 Corinthians 16:13-14.

1 Corinthians 16:13-14

13 Be on your guard; stand firm in the faith; be courageous; be strong. 14 Do everything in love.

We must do everything in love. Love is not just having mercy on someone, it is thinking well of them, doing good for them, having a good attitude about them to their benefit, and helping them do better and be better no matter what you see them do or say. This does not have an attitude that everybody has something bad that needs to be fixed but sometimes even their best can be so much better and love can get them there.

God lavished His love on man through the Old Testament and that is clearly seen in the New Testament how God handled every situation with man. Since God's only begotten son Jesus Christ is the object of God's love and because of Him we are the sons of God. We are also the object of God's love. There are countless occasions in the Old Testament where God saved, healed, delivered, protected, provided, etc., for man, however, none of this was done because man did something to deserve the love of God. This is very important, because when we define love according to whatever condition or event that tickles our fancy, we totally misunderstand what love is.

In the New Testament, God is the object man's love because He loved us first. Jesus gave His life, for us, therefore it is easy to love someone that would be willing to die for you. We have to learn to love the way God loves us. Some of us never consider the way God loves us. For instance, how many times did we tell God we were going to do something and did not? If someone does that to us our first response is to not be satisfied with them? How about praying or studying the word of God, maybe we do a lot of that. How about not obeying His commands in the word of God? How quickly do we forgive people, do we live by faith, and do we fight the enemy (Satan) instead of flesh and blood? God still loves us in spite of our answer to any of those questions. I mentioned this earlier that God loves us from the beginning.

There is nothing we had to do to get God to love us and there is nothing we can do to stop it. No matter what comes our way, Believers cannot be separated from the love of Christ. It does not matter whether it is a situations, a circumstances, people or Satan nothing can separate for the love of God and that is clearly stated in Romans 8:29-39.

Romans 8:29-39

29 For those whom He foreknew [of whom He was [k]aware and [l]loved beforehand], He also destined from the beginning [foreordaining them] to be molded into the image of His Son [and share inwardly His likeness], that He might become the firstborn among many brethren. 30 And those whom He thus foreordained, He also called; and those whom He called, He also justified (acquitted, made righteous, putting them into right standing with Himself). And those whom He justified, He also glorified [raising them to a heavenly dignity and condition or state of being]. 31 What then shall we say to [all] this? If God is for us, who [can be] against us? [Who can be our foe, if God is on our side?] 32 He who did not withhold or spare [even] His own Son but gave Him up for us all, will He not also with Him freely and graciously give us all [other] things? 33 Who shall bring any charge against God's elect [when it is] God Who justifies [that is, Who puts us in right relation to Himself? Who shall come forward and accuse or impeach those whom God has chosen? Will God, Who acquits us?] 34 Who is there to condemn [us]? Will Christ Jesus (the Messiah), Who died, or rather

Who was raised from the dead, Who is at the right hand of God actually pleading as He intercedes for us?35 <u>Who shall ever separate us from Christ's love?</u> Shall suffering and affliction and tribulation? Or calamity and distress? Or persecution or hunger or destitution or peril or sword? 36 Even as it is written, For Thy sake we are put to death all the day long; we are regarded and counted as sheep for the slaughter. 37 Yet amid all these things we are more than conquerors [m]and gain a surpassing <u>victory through Him Who loved us.</u> 38 For I am persuaded beyond doubt (am sure) that neither death nor life, nor angels nor principalities, nor things [n]impending and threatening nor things to come, nor powers,39 Nor height nor depth, nor anything else in all creation will be <u>able to separate us from the love of God</u> which is in Christ Jesus our Lord AMP.

This is an example of God love. Many of us come from dysfunctional families that demonstrated to us as children their version of love. For example, if you know someone that comes from an environment of a battered spouse, they will have no idea of what love really is because there is no example in the home, or if you know someone who consistently call their children or family members bad name they will have no idea of what love is because that does not resemble love. Calling a person ugly causes you to be in direct opposite to what the word of God says about them. Since God made mankind (all of us) in His image and after His likeness to call anybody ugly is calling God ugly because they are in His image and as His likeness. So when they look in the mirror what they see is an image. Now according to God's word they see God. It does not matter who you are if you look in the mirror you see God and we find what God said about that in Genesis 1:26-27.

Genesis 1-26-27

26 And God said, Let us make man in <u>our image</u>, after our likeness: and let them have dominion over the fish of the sea, and over the fowl of the air, and over the cows, and over all the earth, and over every creeping thing that creepeth upon the earth. 27 So God created man in <u>his own image</u>, in the <u>image of God</u> created he him; male and female created he them.

The Hebrew word for image in this passage is *<u>tselem</u>* which means image, likeness (of resemblance). If you have ever called anybody ugly this is something to think about. Just in case you are wondering what that word image means in English the definition according to dictionary.com is a physical likeness or representation of a person, animal, or thing, photographed, painted, sculptured, or otherwise made visible. In addition, the word ugly means according to the same dictionary very unattractive or unpleasant to look at; offensive to the sense of beauty; displeasing in appearance, disagreeable; unpleasant; objectionable: ugly tricks; ugly discords, morally revolting. This is in no way an example of what love is but it is an example of what it is not.

Loving God is more than just saying I love you Lord. But to love God is to know God and abide in Him because God is love. There are many scriptures there that talks about God's love toward man and the world and what our response has been and is to the love of God. One example is in the New Testament that lets us know that our response to the love of God is to love. If we ever want to know God we must chose to love. This can be found in 1 John 4:8 &16.

1 John 4:8 & 16

8 He who does not love does not know God, for God is love. 16 And we have known and believed he love that God has for us. God abides in him, and who abides in love abides in God, and God in him.

God is not looking for love it is already in Him, for He is love and you can never lose by using what is in God. When it comes to winning battles God could just do whatever He needed to do to win but He will not use what is not in Him nor that which is not His character. God wants us to win every battle; therefore He is not going to pick a fight with man just to show us how omnipotent He is. He uses what is in Him to win and love is the attribute that we see Him use over and over again.

The love of God is mentioned in the beginning books of the Bible often, and it is clearly demonstrated by God to all of His creation. God made a covenant with everything that He created and was and is faithful to each and every thing. The power of God is so awesome and it is not containable or stoppable, but it is unchangeable, therefore He can do anything that He wants to do. If He does not do something it is because He chooses not to change what He has already put in place. When He created man He demonstrated His love by putting Adam in the Garden of Eden, the place of his purpose and giving him dominion of everything that He created on the earth. In addition, all of mankind was in Adam and was to flow from Him. God knew and understood this before the foundation of the world. He made a covenant with us as a sign of His commitment to us and His total support of us. Keeping that in mind God created us as an object of the love that is found in Him (Christ). I know that you are wondering how that could be since Adam was on the earth long before Jesus. Let's take a look at John 1:1-5.

1 John 1:1-5

1 In the beginning [before all time] was the Word ([a]Christ), and the Word was with God, and the Word was God [b]Himself. 2 He was present originally with God. 3 All things were made and came into existence through Him; and without Him was not even one thing made that has come into being. 4 In Him was Life, and the Life was the Light of men. 5 And the Light shines on in the darkness, for the darkness has never overpowered it [put it out or absorbed it or appropriated it, and is unreceptive to it].

Therefore, in the beginning was the word of God, which is Christ, He was with God and all things that were made came through Him, without Him nothing came into existence and this includes the first Adam (mankind). Man is an object of God's love through Christ and that was how it was from the beginning.

Chapter 2 – How Is Love Demonstrated?

Our response to God's love is to return that love with our obedience to His commands. God gave Adam everything that he could ever want or need and all He asked Adam to do was to love Him. He expected Adam to reference Him and worship Him by obeying Him. Can you imagine someone loving you so much that they would give you the absolute best of everything that you could ever want or need or even desire in your heart without you ever asking for anything and all you are expected to do is reverence them by your obedience which is a form of worship. God showed us this from the very beginning so that later on when He explained to husbands in the New Testament that they were to love their wives as Christ loves the Church and the wives were to reverence their husband as unto God they would understand. Adam and his wife had a personal relationship with God, they were in the beginning free of sin, they were innocent and knew no sin, and therefore it was possible for God to communicate and fellowship with them personally. This was how God wanted it to be, but after they disobeyed God and ate of the forbidden fruit, they were no longer innocent and this act of sin separated them from God presence and this personal relationship with God was no longer possible as it had once been.

Satan started a war by introducing sin to a sinless people at that time because he knew that God cannot fellowship with evil but God knew that He was going to restore their relationship and He knew that He was going to do it with love by the sacrifice of Jesus Christ; this was an act of love won the war of our restoration. It took some time for the final battle to be won, but that the war was won from the beginning because God does not live in time. We are the heirs of that personal fellowship restoration. Satan did not realize it but all of his efforts to separate us from God were lost. He did not nor can he perform an act of love. Satan is against God and all that God stands for and is. He fights God on every hand, he cannot love, that is not who he is, he can only sin and that is by his choice. He has forever embraced sin. He knows if he presents it to us the way his character really is, we would probably reject it, therefore he uses the tactics of lying, trickery, killing and deceptions. You can never win anything with any of these because the end of all of them is death situations.

It is good to identify what constitute sin. It is anything that contradicts what and who God is, if God had not given Moses the law we would not understand what is sin and what is not sin. Anything that God tells us to do is obviously not sin and when He gave Moses the law that was a standard of do's and don'ts that God gave us, it is a place to mark so that you can know when you missed the mark. Whatever we do against anybody that does not line up with who God is we miss the mark and we sin against God not them.

The definition of sin according to The New Unger's Bible Dictionary is as follows:
"The underlying idea of sin is that of law and of a lawgiver." The lawgiver is God. Hence sin is everything

in the disposition and purpose and conduct of God's moral creatures that is contrary to the expressed will of God.

> *Romans 3:20 - Therefore by the deeds of the law there shall no flesh be justified in his sight: for by the law is the knowledge of sin; Romans 4:15 Because the law worketh wrath: for where no law is, there is no transgression; Romans 7:7 What shall we say then? Is the law sin? God forbid. Nay, I had not known sin, but by the law: for I had not known lust, except the law had said, Thou shalt not covet;*

> *James 4:12 There is one lawgiver, who is able to save and to destroy: who art thou that judgest another? James 4:17 Therefore to him that knoweth to do good, and doeth it not, to him it is sin.*

The sinfulness of sin lies in the fact that it is against God, even when the wrong we do is to others or ourselves.

> *Genesis 39:9 There is none greater in this house than I; neither hath he kept back any thing from me but thee, because thou art his wife: how then can I do this great wickedness, and sin against God? Psalm 51:4 Against thee, thee only, have I sinned, and done this evil in thy sight: that thou mightest be justified when thou speakest, and be clear when thou judgest.*

The being and law of God are perfectly harmonious, for "**God is love**." The sum of all **the commandments likewise** is love; sin in its nature is egotism and selfishness. Self is put in the place of God.

> *Romans 15:3 For even Christ pleased not himself; but, as it is written, The reproaches of them that reproached thee fell on me; 1 Corinthians 13:5 Doth not behave itself unseemly, seeketh not her own, is not easily provoked, thinketh no evil; 2 Timothy 3:2 For men shall be lovers of their own selves, covetous, boasters, proud, blasphemers, disobedient to parents, unthankful, unholy, 2 Timothy 3:4 Traitors, heady, highminded, lovers of pleasures more than lovers of God;*

> *2 Thessalonians 2:3 Let no man deceive you by any means: for that day shall not come, except there come a falling away first, and that man of sin be revealed, the son of perdition; 4 Who opposeth and exalteth himself above all that is called God, or that is worshipped; so that he as God sitteth in the temple of God, shewing himself that he is God.*

Selfishness (not pure self-love, or the exaggeration of it, but in opposition to it) is at the bottom of all disobedience, and it becomes hostility to God when it collides with His law."

God is constantly and consistently bringing us to the point where we look and act like Him. When we look at all that God did as it relates to man we can understand that God was demonstrating the love of a father and a husband to His people. At this point in the Old Testament we can only see Him clearly as Father and Husband, but later in the New Testament we can see His love demonstrated as Savior, Lord and King. Yes, God was Savior, Lord and King to man in the Old Testament but it was not easily recognized because man was not able to have a personal intimate relationship with God, we had to go through the Priesthood of Aaron (with Aaron as high Priest) and those in the Levitical Priesthood, we had to depend on them to use the blood of animals to get to God for us and for them to bring the message back from God to us. But now because Jesus Christ our High Priest has won for us a personal audience with God by His own personal blood and it is forever because the Priesthood in the order of Melchizedek which is the order of His priesthood has no beginning and no end.

There are many instances of God's demonstration of His love to man in the Old Testament and we will cover several just to get understanding, Let us start with Adam God strategically put everything in place before he turned it over to Adam. You may ask how God demonstrated himself as a husband when there was no woman at that time. There was a woman at that time she was just inside of Adam. Adam had the male and female component in him, remember, God did not create another Adam when she came on the scene, He took her out of Him and separated his womb from him. When God formed man, he formed mankind male and female, in the beginning we see in Genesis 2:7 and also in Genesis 1:27.

Genesis 2:7 And the LORD God formed man of the dust of the ground, and breathed into his nostrils the breath of life; and man became a living soul. Genesis 1:27 So God created man in his own image, in the image of God created he him; male and female created he them.

God did this at one time, He did not do it separately, He even called them both Adam we see that in Genesis 5:2.

Genesis 5:2

Male and female created he them; and blessed them, and called their name Adam, in the day when they were created.

Later, when God presented all of creations to Adam to see if he would pick one to help him and he did not pick any of them, then God took the man with the womb from him and presented her to him. It is the intention of God that they become one again and operates as one since Adam was operating as one person from the beginning because all that he needed to function was in him.We see the account of this in Genesis 2:19-24.

Genesis 2:19-24

19 And out of the ground the LORD God formed every beast of the field, and every fowl of the air; and brought them unto Adam to see what he would call them: and whatsoever Adam called every living creature, that was the name thereof.

> *20 And Adam gave names to all cattle, and to the fowl of the air, and to every beast of the field; but for Adam there was not found an help meet for him. 21 And the LORD God caused a deep sleep to fall upon Adam, and he slept: and he took one of his ribs, and closed up the flesh instead thereof; 22 And the rib, which the LORD God had taken from man, made he a woman, and brought her unto the man. 23 And Adam said, This is now bone of my bones, and flesh of my flesh: she shall be called Woman, because she was taken out of Man. 24 Therefore shall a man leave his father and his mother, and shall cleave unto his wife: and they shall be one flesh.*

God calls them both Adam, but Adam called her woman and this was the beginning of the split. The word woman in the Hebrew is ishshah which means woman, wife, female, woman (opposite of man), wife (woman married to a man), female (of animals), each, every (pronoun). We are still talking about being the wife of God and the object of His love.

Chapter 3 - God Used Love to Win the War

God knew that man would sin yet He loved man. God knew that man would choose not to love Him, as demonstrated by man's disobedience to Him and man's obedience to the serpent. Yet, God had a plan that was motivated and executed in love. If you notice God's reaction to their sin was that of a good Father, He corrected them, He had them deal with the consequences and He covered them. Then He proceeded to show His love from generation to generation until we see the ultimate sacrifice He would make for us in love to bring us back into His presence, the birth of Jesus Christ. God won the war of saving man with love and because of His love for man. We have a covenant with God that is established in love. He would never give up on us; He would never stop the process of bringing us back to His expected end. Moses explained the love of God to the children of Israel in Deuteronomy 7:9.

Deuteronomy 7:9

Understand, therefore, that the LORD your God is indeed God. He is the faithful God who keeps his covenant for a thousand generations and lavishes his unfailing love on those who love him and obey his commands.

The Hebrew word for love in this passage is 'ahab which means - to love, (Qal) human love for another, includes family, and sexual human appetite for objects such as food, drink, sleep, wisdom, human love for or to God, act of being a friend, lover (participle), friend (participle), God's love toward man, to individual men, to people Israel, to righteousness, (Niphal) lovely (participle), loveable (participle) (Piel) friends, lovers (fig. of adulterers), to like.

This is mentioned in the Old Testament that love never fail, this passage calls God love an unfailing love. John also mentioned what God was willing and able to do to save us from being separated from Him forever, we were an estranged wife that needed to come to him through the blood of animals, but John restated the love that God has toward all of His creation in John 3:16.

John 3:16

For God so loved the world, that he gave his only begotten Son, that whosoever believeth in him should not perish, but have everlasting life.

Since God created the world it is understandable that He wants to lavish His love on the world. I was saved as a child and I was taught that this passage was only talking about people, it includes people, but this is much more than just the people. The word world in the Greek is kosmos whichmeans an apt and harmonious arrangement or constitution, order, government, ornament, decoration, adornment, i.e. the arrangement of the stars, 'the heavenly hosts', as the ornament of the heavens.

In 1 Pet. 3:3, the world, the universe, the circle of the earth, the earth, the inhabitants of the earth, men, the human family, the ungodly multitude; the whole mass of men alienated from God, and therefore hostile to the cause of Christ, world affairs, the aggregate of things earthly, the whole circle of earthly goods, endowments riches, advantages, pleasures, etc., which although hollow and frail and fleeting, stir desire, seduce from God and are obstacles to the cause of Christ, any aggregate or general collection of particulars of any sort the Gentiles as contrasted to the Jews (See Romans 11:12, etc.)

God loves all of this and more, what is so wonderful, these things or people did not have to put in an application to God for consideration of His love, He just loved them! John goes on to explain that God sent His only Son to save the world not to condemn it. This is His demonstration of love of God, He did not say I love you but His actions demonstrated who He is, He cannot show anything but love since He is love. John further says in John 3:17.

John 3:17

For God sent not his Son into the world to condemn the world; but that the world through him might be saved.

What an act of love, most of the time when people do evil things to other people they want retribution, by law through the court system or by direct payment in like kind or by financial satisfaction. Therefore, even when God is unpleased with us He still loves us, and everything that he does is in love.

Micah 7:18-19

Where is another God like you, who pardons the guilt of the remnant, overlooking the sins of his special people? You will not stay angry with your people forever, because you delight in showing unfailing love. 19 He will turn again, he will have compassion upon us; he will subdue our iniquities; and thou wilt cast all their sins into the depths of the sea.

God love for His people is not limited to just a chosen few, some of us think that God loves particular people but not everybody in the group, many believers have been convinced that God likes them and has saved them but He does not love them like He does some others for whatever reason, but God is love and it is not possible for Him to kick anybody out of the covenant. Notice what the queen of Sheba said to King Solomon in 1 Kings 10:9.

1 Kings 10: 9

Blessed be the LORD thy God, which delighted in thee, to set thee on the throne of Israel: because the LORD loved Israel for ever, therefore made he thee king, to do judgment and justice.

Israel is the entire nation of Israel; this is how God is demonstrating how to love to all of us. The Hebrew word for love in this passage is '**ahabah** which means love, human love for human object, of man toward man, of man toward himself, between man and woman, sexual desire, God's love to His people. This definition includes God's love for his people. The love God has for His people is not negotiable, it does not matter what our circumstances, conditions, situations, problems etc. are His love remains the same.

From the beginning with Adam from time to time you will see the love of God demonstrated over and over again down through the ages. Isaiah 63:7, talks about the lovingkindness of God as in regards to God's love for Israel.

Isaiah 63:7

I will mention the lovingkindnesses of the LORD, and the praises of the LORD, according to all that the LORD hath bestowed on us, and the great goodness toward the house of Israel, which he hath bestowed on them according to his mercies, and according to the multitude of his lovingkindnesses.

The Hebrew word for lovingkindness is **checed** which means goodness, kindness, faithfulness, a reproach, shame. The KJV translates this word as mercy, kindness, lovingkindness, goodness, kindly, merciful, favour, good, goodliness, pity, reproach, wicked thing. It is clear that goodness is what is being said here. In addition, the goodness toward the house of Israel and He expressed His lovingkindness multitudes of times just because He loved them.

Chapter 4 - People Winning Battles with Love

The characteristics of love are best defined in 1 Corinthians 13:4-7.

1 Corinthians 13:4-8

Love endures long and is patient and kind; love never is envious nor boils over with jealousy, is not boastful or vainglorious, does not display itself haughtily. 5 It is not conceited (arrogant and inflated with pride); it is not rude (unmannerly) and does not act unbecomingly. Love (God's love in us) does not insist on its own rights or its own way, for it is not self-seeking; it is not touchy or fretful or resentful; it takes no account of the evil done to it [it pays no attention to a suffered wrong]. 6 It does not rejoice at injustice and unrighteousness, but rejoices when right and truth prevail. 7 Love bears up under anything and everything that comes, is ever ready to believe the best of every person, its hopes are fadeless under all circumstances, and it endures everything [without weakening]. 8 Love never fails [never fades out or becomes obsolete or comes to an end]. As for prophecy ([d]the gift of interpreting the divine will and purpose), it will be fulfilled and pass away; as for tongues, they will be destroyed and cease; as for knowledge, it will pass away [it will lose its value and be superseded by truth. AMP

There are many people that are examples of winning battles with the love of God as defined in 1 Corinthians 13. The person never said to the persons "I love you" but their actions toward the people that were harming them demonstrated the love of God. It is easy to love people that love you but the real test of love being a lifestyle for you is how you treat your enemies. Let us take a look at a few people that lived a lifestyle of love.

Daniel - This is a story that most bible readers know.

Daniel was a businessman, so this is extremely important for those of you who work in corporate America, own your own business, or work in a business environment with coworkers that may or may not like you. Daniel's coworkers were jealous of his position and the honor that he received from the king, because of that honor they set a trap for him and desired that he be killed. The account of this is found in Daniel 6:3-4.

Daniel 6:3-4

Then this Daniel was preferred above the presidents and princes, because an excellent spirit was in him; and the king thought to set him over the whole realm. 4 Then the presidents and princes sought to find occasion against Daniel concerning the kingdom; but they could find none occasion nor fault; forasmuch as he was faithful, neither was there any error or fault found in him.

Daniel knew that they did not like him but he said not a word against them. He knew that they were talking about him still he said nothing. His coworkers looked for something to accuse him of but they found nothing, then they decided to use his love for God to trap him. The account of this is found in Daniel 6:5-8.

Daniel 6:5-8

5 Then said these men, We shall not find any occasion against this Daniel, except we find it against him concerning the law of his God. 6 Then these presidents and princes assembled together to the king, and said thus unto him, King Darius, live for ever. 7 All the presidents of the kingdom, the governors, and the princes, the counsellors, and the captains, have consulted together to establish a royal statute, and to make a firm decree, that whosoever shall ask a petition of any God or man for thirty days, save of thee, O king, he shall be cast into the den of lions.

They knew that Daniel was accustomed to praying three times a day and they knew that Daniel would not compromise his relationship with God. They knew that Daniel was not going to wait thirty days or any day to pray to God. Daniel did not go to the king or complain about the trap that they has set for him because he knew that he was not going to give up his prayer time and he decided to trust God. As their plot unfolded as reported in Daniel 6:8-10.

Daniel 6:8-10

8 Now, O king, establish the decree, and sign the writing, that it be not changed, according to the law of the Medes and Persians, which altereth not. 9 Wherefore king Darius signed the writing and the decree. 10 Now when Daniel knew that the writing was signed, he went into his house; and his windows being open in his chamber toward Jerusalem, he kneeled upon his knees three times a day, and prayed, and gave thanks before his God, as he did aforetime.

In the mist of knowing all that he knew about what was happening to him, he continued to love them. In fact everything that Daniel did toward them was in love, He knew what they were doing was meant to destroy him but he still did not say a word. His coworkers followed him home to spy on him so that they could report that to the king and get Daniel thrown into the den of lions in Daniel 6:11-15.

Daniel 6:11-15

11 Then these men assembled, and found Daniel praying and making 12 Then they came near, and spake before the king concerning the king's decree; Hast thou not signed a decree, that every man that shall ask a petition of any God or man within thirty days, save of thee, O king, shall be cast into the den of lions? The king answered and said, The thing is true, according to the law of the Medes 13 Then answered they and said before the king, That Daniel, which is of the children of the captivity of Judah, regardeth not thee, O king, nor the decree that thou hast signed, but maketh his petition three times a day. 14 Then the king, when he heard these words, was sore displeased with himself, and set his heart on Daniel to deliver him: and he laboured till the going down of the sun to deliver him. 15 Then these men assembled unto the king, and said unto the king, Know, O king, that the law of the Medes and Persians is, That no decree nor statute which the king establisheth may be changed.

Daniel was loved by the king because he was a good steward and excellent in spirit and the king did not want to put him in the den of lions, he even blamed himself for signing that decree, he tried to save Daniel but his own law cannot be changed. What he did not realize is that the love of God cannot be changed. Daniel exemplified love toward everyone involved in this matter. He did not get angry with the king whom he had served faithfully. He did not complain that this was a poor reward for his faithful service, nor did he try to defend himself from the trap of his coworkers. He loved the people and trusted God. That is one of the reasons that we struggle so with anger and offense when people do things to us. We trust them instead of loving them. God never said to trust them, he said to love them and trust Him. If Daniel had trusted the people instead of loving them he would not have positioned himself to win. Since his trust was in God and not the people it was easier for him to not get angry with them or offended by their attack. They all distrusted and dishonored Daniel but he still loved them. It appears that his love for his coworkers was his ticket to the lion's den, but this is not the end of the story. Daniel finds himself on his way to the den of lions in Daniel 6:16-17.

Daniel 6:16-17

Then the king commanded, and they brought Daniel, and cast him into the den of lions. Now the king spake and said unto Daniel, Thy God whom thou servest continually, he will deliver thee. 17 And a stone was brought, and laid upon the mouth of the den; and the king sealed it with his own signet, and with the signet of his lords; that the purpose might not be changed concerning Daniel.

It would seem if Daniel had lost but love never fails. We see what happened in the next in verses.

Daniel 6:19-22

19 Then the king arose very early in the morning, and went in haste unto the den of lions. 20 And when he came to the den, he cried with a lamentable voice unto Daniel: and the king spake and said to Daniel, O Daniel, servant of the living God, is thy God, whom thou servest continually, able to deliver thee from the lions?

> **21 Then said Daniel unto the king, O king, live for ever. 22 My God hath sent his angel, and hath shut the lions' mouths, that they have not hurt me: forasmuch as before him innocency was found in me; and also before thee, O king, have I done no hurt.**

You say now, there was no mention of love in this passage but what Daniel did were the characteristics of love that I gave you in 1 Corinthians. 13. No matter what happened to Daniel he did nothing to harm them in speech or deed. He used the love of God to win. This is what we have to do also. We have to believe in and trust God no matter what is happening. The next verse in Daniel says:

Daniel 6:23

> **Then was the king exceeding glad for him, and commanded that they should take Daniel up out of the den. So Daniel was taken up out of the den, and no manner of hurt was found upon him, because he believed in his God.**

Now the king realize what had happened, this was a trap that they had set for Daniel, since he seemed to be the only one adversely affected by what they did. The deceived the king and did not tell him of their motive, they purposed to get the lions to kill Daniel because they could find any fault in him. As a result, death for them was found at the end of what they did in Daniel 6:24.

Daniel 6:24

And the king commanded, and they brought those men which had accused Daniel, and they cast them into the den of lions, them, their children, and their wives; and the lions had the mastery of them, and brake all their bones in pieces or ever they came at the bottom of the den. Now God's power and love is on display for everyone to see. When you win with love you win big see what happened in Daniel 6:25-27.

Daniel 6:25-27

Then king Darius wrote unto all people, nations, and languages, that dwell in all the earth; Peace be multiplied unto you. 26 I make a decree, That in every dominion of my kingdom men tremble and fear before the God of Daniel: for he is the living God, and stedfast for ever, and his kingdom that which shall not be destroyed, and his dominion shall be even unto the end. 27 He delivereth and rescueth, and he worketh signs and wonders in heaven and in earth, who hath delivered Daniel from the power of the lions.

Look at how big Daniel won in Daniel 6:28.

Daniel 6:28

So this Daniel prospered in the reign of Darius, and in the reign of Cyrus the Persian.

Even though the scripture did not say that Daniel loved his coworkers, he did indeed show those characteristics of love. We know from 1 Corinthians 13, what love really looks like. Daniel did those things. Love is not being jealous or envious. Daniel was neither, but his coworkers were. Daniel endured long with them; he was at the meeting where they set him up to be put into the den lions. Daniel knew that he was chosen over all of them to lead them, he was not inflated with pride, he did not insist on his rights, he was not fretful or resentful and he paid no attention to the wrong that he suffered at their hands.

Joseph

He was the 11th son of Jacob, his mother was Rachael and his mother has one other son Benjamin, the 12th son, the two of them had the same mother, but the other 10 sons of Jacobs had different mothers. All of the brothers were the sons of Jacob. Jacob had 12 sons and 1 daughter. They were one big blended family. This is a very special case because the people that Joseph had to love first were his biological brothers. They were not the only ones, but they were the first ones that he needed protection from. I am not sure at what point Joseph started trusting God, he loved his brother but he trusted God. His brothers hated him because of the love their father had for him and for the dream that God had given him that his brothers would serve him at some time in the future. Joseph did not ask for anything from his father but he was the one that received the coat of many colors. If you have ever had any problems with family members that for whatever reason cannot celebrate you, love you, be fair to you or not willing to treat you as they do other family members this love story will bless your life. Let us look at what happened to Joseph and how he use love to win the battles in Genesis 37:2-4.

Genesis 37:2-4

These are the generations of Jacob. Joseph, being seventeen years old, was feeding the flock with his brethren; and the lad was with the sons of Bilhah, and with the sons of Zilpah, his father's wives: and Joseph brought unto his father their evil report. 3 Now Israel loved Joseph more than all his children, because he was the son of his old age: and he made him a coat of many colours. 4 And when his brethren saw that their father loved him more than all his brethren, they hated him, and could not speak peaceably unto him.

Joseph loved them, he knew that they hated him but he still loved them all. The scripture mentions here that they could not speak peaceably unto him. He did not let that stop him from speaking peaceable to them. In addition to having to listen to them complain, criticize and whatever else they had to say that was not peaceable to him God gave him a dream.

Genesis 37:5-8

And Joseph dreamed a dream, and he told it his brethren: and they hated him yet the more. 6 And he said unto them, Hear, I pray you, this dream which I have dreamed: 7 For, behold, we were binding sheaves in the field, and, lo, my sheaf arose, and also stood upright; and, behold, your sheaves stood round about, and made obeisance to my sheaf. 8 And his brethren said to him, Shalt thou indeed reign over us? or shalt thou indeed have dominion over us? And they hated him yet the more for his dreams, and for his words.

Now they hate him even more for his dream sake. This must have been very traumatic for Joseph, he did not ask to be born, he did not ask to be his father favorite, he did not ask God for the dream, yet he was hated for what he was to other people. He took a position of love and he stayed on course with that. I believe that God gave both Daniel and Joseph special help to love the folk that were trying to kill them.

That not the end of Joseph's dreams, he had another dream and by now they were so outdone they begin to envy him. Joseph shared his latest dream with his family in Genesis 37:9-11.

Genesis 37:9-11

And he dreamed yet another dream, and told it his brethren, and said, Behold, I have dreamed a dream more; and, behold, the sun and the moon and the eleven stars made obeisance to me. 10 And he told it to his father, and to his brethren: and his father rebuked him, and said unto him, What is this dream that thou hast dreamed?

Shall I and thy mother and thy brethren indeed
come to bow down ourselves to thee to the earth?
11 And his brethren envied him; but his father
observed the saying.

Notice, Joseph is sharing his dream; his love for them
has not change. He is not boasting about the dream or his
God given assignment. Joseph wants them to be happy
for him, he wants them to celebrate with him, he wants
his family to share in his dreams but his brothers refused.
Joseph was patient with them, and he had no idea of how
much they hated him, but he knew that they were not
pleased with him at all. He was not fretful or resentful
and he paid no attention to the wrong that he suffered at
their hands already.

There came a time when their father sent Joseph to check
on his brothers because they were feeding the sheep in
another place away from home. Joseph went looking for
them in the place where were supposed to be and did not
find them. There was a certain man there that told Joseph
where they had gone. We find that in Genesis 37:16-21.

Genesis 37:16-21

16 And he said, I seek my brethren: tell me, I
pray thee, where they feed their flocks. 17 And
the man said, They are departed hence; for I
heard them say, Let us go to Dothan. And
Joseph went after his brethren, and found them
in Dothan. 18 And when they saw him afar off,
even before he came near unto them, they
conspired against him to slay him. 19 And they

> *said one to another, Behold, this dreamer*
> *cometh. 20 Come now therefore, and let us slay*
> *him, and cast him into some pit, and we will say,*
> *some evil beast hath devoured him: and we shall*
> *see what will become of his dreams. 21 And*
> *Reuben heard it, and he delivered him out of*
> *their hands; and said, Let us not kill him.*

Treating Joseph poorly at some point was not enough for them. They wanted to remove him from the planet. They wanted to kill Joseph and get rid of him forever. Joseph was already dealing with their rejection of him, He was already an outcast to them, they did not want him to be a part of what they were doing because they knew that if he found out that they were not doing what they needed to be doing he would tell their father and they would get in trouble. As they made plans to kill Joseph, Reuben came up with an alternate plan to put him in a pit and somehow get him back to their father, but he did not tell the rest of his brothers of his plans to return him to their father. The account of what happened then in found in Genesis 37:22.

Genesis 37:22

And Reuben said unto them, Shed no blood, but cast him into this pit that is in the wilderness, and lay no hand upon him; that he might rid him out of their hands, to deliver him to his father again. What happened next is something that Joseph had not expected but through all of this he never said a word to his father or to them about their attitude toward him. Joseph never started an argument or a fight and he never expressed any anger to his father about what was happening to him. What happened next is so interesting because when people do these kind of things to us we want to do what they did to us back to them and that will cause us to lose the battle every time. When Joseph arrived look at what they did in Genesis 37:23-24.

Genesis 37:23-24

And it came to pass, when Joseph was come unto his brethren, that they stript Joseph out of his coat, his coat of many colours that was on him; 24 And they took him, and cast him into a pit: and the pit was empty, there was no water in it.

This was their brother and what they did was not a problem for them at all. In fact they sat down to eat, laugh and joke, but did not give him any food. If you remember, this is what happened to Jesus at the cross, they stripped him of his coat before they nailed him to the cross.

When Reuben returned they had already sold their brother into slavery for twenty pieces of silver.

Genesis 37:25-28

25 And they sat down to eat bread: and they lifted up their eyes and looked, and, behold, a company of Ishmaelites came from Gilead with their camels bearing spicery and balm and myrrh, going to carry it down to Egypt. 26 And

> *Judah said unto his brethren, What profit is it if we slay our brother, and conceal his blood? 27 Come, and let us sell him to the Ishmeelites, and let not our hand be upon him; for he is our brother and our flesh. And his brethren were content. 28 Then there passed by Midianites merchantmen; and they drew and lifted up Joseph out of the pit, and sold Joseph to the Ishmeelites for twenty pieces of silver: and they brought Joseph into Egypt.*

Reuben rented his clothes because he knows that there is nothing he can do to save his brother at this point. God was planning to use Joseph to save his family in a time of famine and to plant them where they could grow into a nation, but Joseph did not know that. He just continued to love his brothers and trust God. Judah was the one who came up with the idea to sell him, yet Judah had to be saved because he was the one that would be in the bloodline of Jesus Christ. Love was what was needed to stay focus and stay on point when everything is screaming at you and all you can do is pray. You cannot say anything. That is exactly what Joseph did. He said not a word to anybody during the entire process. Joseph did not think that he would ever see his family again. That must have been a very hard place to come from but he never took the opportunity to operate the way they did. He loved his brothers and his parents but he never said a word about the wrong that was done to him.

Now his brothers have to go back to their father and tell him a lie about what happened. That is one reason their father needed Joseph to tell him what they were doing because they had some character issues in this area. Their father was very grieved at the loss of his son and it was not easy for him to get over the loss of Joseph. Knowing exactly what they had done they tried to comfort their father but he could not be comforted. The scripture reports what happened in Genesis 37:34-35.

Genesis 37:34-35

And Jacob rent his clothes, and put sackcloth upon his loins, and mourned for his son many days. 35 And all his sons and all his daughters rose up to comfort him; but he refused to be comforted; and he said, For I will go down into the grave unto my son mourning. Thus his father wept for him.

Joseph's life took a hard turn and he had even more opportunity to demonstrate the love of God during his process of growth. He is now confronted again with doing his best for someone and they lie on him and cause him to have to take another hard turn. We can see what happened in Genesis 37:36.

Genesis 37:36

And the Midianites sold him into Egypt unto Potiphar, an officer of Pharaoh's, and captain of the guard.

He is now at the mercy of his slave owner Potiphar. The LORD was with Joseph and he prospered. Potiphar was so impressed with his stewardship he made Joseph overseer over his house to the point that he did not even know what he had.

Genesis 39:2-6

2 And the LORD was with Joseph, and he was a prosperous man; and he was in the house of his master the Egyptian. 3 And his master saw that the LORD was with him, and that the LORD made all that he did to prosper in his hand. 4 And Joseph found grace in his sight, and he served him: and he made him overseer over his house, and all that he had he put into his hand. 5 And it came to pass from the time that he had made him overseer in his house, and over all that he had, that the LORD blessed the Egyptian's house for Joseph's sake; and the blessing of the LORD was upon all that he had in the house, and in the field. 6 And he left all that he had in Joseph's hand; and he knew not ought he had, save the bread which he did eat. And Joseph was a goodly person, and well favoured.

Even as a slave Joseph continued to love, he had to make an adjustment of accepting what he was doing and where he was and giving his best which was all he ever did. He had done nothing to deserve this grief and pain but did not allow it to make him angry, bitter, or complacent. He loved the work and the people. He was a good steward just as Daniel was of all that he put his hands to. He was no longer in the position of being the favorite in the house of his father. He was no longer in a position of honor but he never said a word and no one knew what had happened to him because he continued to love his family and trust God.

Joseph was doing so well in Potiphar's house, Potiphar trusted him to take care of all of his business. However, Potiphar's wife wanted Joseph but he refused to dishonor his master. Notice that Joseph was explaining to her about sinning against her husband and God. She was not interested in that because she had already made up her mind to sin against her husband. Joseph knew that was not something that he could do and she grabs his clothes and they came off and he ran. At first he was confronted with keeping his mouth shut, now he has to run. Joseph must have been lonely. The bible did not say that he had anyone close to him. He must have wanted a wife, someone to love and someone to love him, but was not the way to satisfy that need. It is difficult sometimes to obey God but it is always possible. We can see what happened in Genesis 39:7-13.

Genesis 39:7-13

7 And it came to pass after these things, that his master's wife cast her eyes upon Joseph; and she said, Lie with me. 8 But he refused, and said unto his master's wife, Behold, my master wotteth not what is with me in the house, and he hath committed all that he hath to my hand; 9 There is none greater in this house than I; neither hath he kept back any thing from me but thee, because thou art his wife: how then can I do this great wickedness, and sin against God?

> **10 And it came to pass, as she spake to Joseph day by day, that he hearkened not unto her, to lie by her, or to be with her. 11 And it came to pass about this time, that Joseph went into the house to do his business; and there was none of the men of the house there within. 12 And she caught him by his garment, saying, Lie with me: and he left his garment in her hand, and fled, and got him out. 13 And it came to pass, when she saw that he had left his garment in her hand, and was fled forth,**

In her anger and scorn, she accused Joseph falsely of doing what she had invited him to do and as a result Joseph ended up in jail. Potiphar put Joseph in jail for what he did not do. Joseph demonstrated love with both of them. He had done everything he could to make their lives more prosperous but that was not enough. Joseph's integrity and his character should have been enough for his master, but it was not. This was yet another opportunity for Joseph to become angry and bitter, he could have made a decision not to love people anymore, but he did not do that. He assessed his situation in the prison and began to be a good steward there even though he was now a prisoner.

What happened to Joseph was amazing, he was winning as a slave, and he was winning as a prisoner because the LORD was with him. When you live a lifestyle of love, you have positioned yourself for the LORD to abide with you and that is what Joseph did. The LORD abided with him everywhere he went and in all of his circumstances. Once he reached the prison he found himself in another position of favor. The LORD loved him also. It was not a one way street. Joseph set his will to operate in God's character of love and kept that position no matter what came his way. His favor is seen in the prison in Genesis 39:21-23.

Genesis 39:21-23

But the LORD was with Joseph, and shewed him mercy, and gave him favour in the sight of the keeper of the prison. 22 And the keeper of the prison committed to Joseph's hand all the prisoners that were in the prison; and whatsoever they did there, he was the doer of it. 23 The keeper of the prison looked not to any thing that was under his hand; because the LORD was with him, and that which he did, the LORD made it to prosper.

The prison keeper left Joseph's space unlocked, he did not lock anything that was under Joseph's hand. His character and integrity was intact, but he was still a prisoner. This was another opportunity for Joseph to see the importance of winning with love. No matter what happened to him he continued to love people and did not despise those who wronged him and he paid no attention to the wrong that was done to him. He kept on believing that someday he would be free. His hope was fadeless under all circumstances, and it endures everything without weakening. He never gave up on God; he trusted God and he never gave up on himself. Running away from things is not the answer, it may make you feel better but it does not solve anything. What Joseph had to go through had nothing to do with how he felt, because his victories had nothing to do with feelings, however, it had everything to do with his response to the situations presented to him. Joseph had one more encounter before he was finally delivered from his process and came into his purpose. He interpreted the dreams of two of the prisoners. One of them was returned to the king and Joseph asked him to help him get out of the prison because he had done nothing to be there, but that person forgot about Joseph's request and it was two more years before he could get out. This was another opportunity for Joseph to give up but he did not.

There came a time when the king needed a person like Joseph to interpret his dream. The prisoner that forgot about Joseph remembers him now and the king sent for him. This was the beginning of Joseph's being free of all of the drama that he had experienced since the time his brothers sold him.

Genesis 41:12-14

12 And there was there with us a young man, an Hebrew, servant to the captain of the guard; and we told him, and he interpreted to us our dreams; to each man according to his dream he did interpret. 13 And it came to pass, as he interpreted to us, so it was; me he restored unto mine office, and him he hanged. 14 Then Pharaoh sent and called Joseph, and they brought him hastily out of the dungeon: and he shaved himself, and changed his raiment, and came in unto Pharaoh.

Let us take a quick review of what happened with Joseph.

Joseph's principle was to believe God and realize this is working for my good and the good of God. God wants to use me to do what He knows is best. It is not easy to do, but when you do all you can do you have to trust God even when you do not understand what is going on. Joseph loved his family in spite of what they thought of him. Sometimes we spend much time trying to get people to love us, especially some of our sisters and brothers in Christ. Jesus understood the importance of loving our brothers in Christ and He admonished us to do that regardless of what they do to us, we can confront them if we have problems with them but we do not have any opportunity not to love them.

We cannot even bring an offering or gift to God if we have an issue with our brother in Christ. Jesus said that in Matthew 5:23-24.

Matthew 5:23-24

Therefore if thou bring thy gift to the altar, and there rememberest that thy brother ought against thee; 24 Leave there thy gift before the altar, and go thy way; first be reconciled to thy brother, and then come and offer thy gift.

There are absolutely no conditions where we can have an excuse for not loving our brother. I know now you are wondering what to do if your brother does not want to admit that he wronged you, then you apologize to him as if you did the wrong because love is who God is, He is love and He wants us to have His character and therefore, He gives us no excuse for not loving Him or our brothers, in addition to all of that you and I need to have God accept our offering and gifts to Him. The word of God further tells us this in Matthew 5:22.

Matthew 5:22

But I say unto you, That whosoever is angry with his brother without a cause shall be in danger of the judgment: and whosoever shall say to his brother, Raca, shall be in danger of the council: but whosoever shall say, Thou fool, shall be in danger of hell fire.

You cannot even say you love God if you do not love your brother this is found in 1 John 4:20.

1 John 4:20

Whoever claims to love God yet hates a brother or sister is a liar. For whoever does not love their brother and sister, whom they have seen, cannot love God, whom they have not seen.

Joseph showed us how to do this, because this is what he did. What his brothers did had to be traumatic for him; look at some of the things his brothers and others did:

● His brothers hated him just because his father loved him -*Genesis 37:4 4 And when his brethren saw that their father loved him more than all his brethren, they hated him, and could not speak peaceably unto him.*

- His brothers hated and envied him for the gift God had given him *-Genesis 37:11 11 And his brethren envied him; but his father observed the saying.*

- His brothers planned to kill him *-Genesis 37:20 Come now therefore, and let us slay him, and cast him into some pit, and we will say, Some evil beast hath devoured him: and we shall see what will become of his dreams.*

- They threw him in a pit buried him *-Gen 37:22 22 And Reuben said unto them, Shed no blood, but cast him into this pit that is in the wilderness, and lay no hand upon him; that he might rid him out of their hands, to deliver him to his father again.*

- They stripped him of his coat *-Gen 37:23 23 And it came to pass, when Joseph was come unto his brethren, that they stript Joseph out of his coat, his coat of many colours that was on him;*

- They sold him into slavery *-Gen 37:25 25 And they sat down to eat bread: and they lifted up their eyes and looked, and, behold, a company of Ishmeelites came from Gilead with their camels bearing spicery and balm and myrrh, going to carry it down to Egypt.*

- He was sold at least two times. Ishmaelite merchants from Gilead were with the Midianites merchants in route to Egypt. His brothers sold him to the Midianites.

They sold him to an Egyptian and they sold him to Potiphar *-Genesis 37:28 28 Then there passed by Midianites merchantmen; and they drew and lifted up Joseph out of the pit, and sold Joseph to the Ishmaelite for twenty pieces of silver: and they brought Joseph into Egypt. KJV Genesis 37:36 36 And the Midianites sold him into Egypt unto Potiphar, an officer of Pharaoh's, and captain of the guard.*

● Potiphar wife lied on him

● Potiphar put him in Prison

● The prisoner that promised to remember him did not

Remember that God said if you love me you will keep my commandments. If you notice Joseph obeyed God, he loved God, his family and the people in his life. He had to spend much time in prayer. Since he had no one else he must have talked to God all of the time. When you go through whatever you have to go through it is good to spend a lot of time in prayer and fasting. There were times when Joseph has to do some involuntary fasting, especially those three days that he was in the pit. It seems as if nobody loved him except God and sometimes it may seem that way to us as well. Nevertheless, he won in the battle. The war was already won because God knew that He wanted to Joseph to save his family, but Joseph had to go through his process in order to qualify and complete his assignment so the battles were in his life not the life of his family, not in the lives of his friends, not the life of his masters, not in the life of

Pharaoh, but in his life and he won them all by loving God, being obedient and loving people thus exhibiting that special character of love that only comes from God.

Pharaoh had a dream and no one could interpret it except Joseph, then Joseph was able to tell him how to administer the dream and manage the assets that God had put in Pharaoh's hands. Joseph knew that he could do the job but he did not even suggest himself. He was not boastful or self seeking. He suggested to Pharaoh to choose someone to take care of it for him. Pharaoh chose Joseph for the assignment and gave God the glory for all that he saw in Joseph, he said to Joseph "Forasmuch as God hath shown you all this, there is none so discreet and wise as you are".

Joseph could not have imagined that God had planned this for him and his family. So none of us can say that he did it for a reward, he was rewarded royally but he did it because he loved unconditionally and he trusted God. You can't beat God loving because God is love. We see Joseph's blessing in Genesis 41:37-45.

Genesis 41:37-45

37 And the thing was good in the eyes of Pharaoh, and in the eyes of all his servants. 38 And Pharaoh said unto his servants, Can we find such a one as this is, a man in whom the Spirit of God is? 39 And Pharaoh said unto Joseph, Forasmuch as God hath shewed thee all this, there is none so discreet and wise as thou art: 40 Thou shalt be over my house, and according unto thy word shall all my people be ruled: only in the throne will I be greater than thou. 41 And Pharaoh said unto Joseph, See, I have set thee over all the land of Egypt. 42 And Pharaoh took off his ring from his hand, and put it upon Joseph's hand, and arrayed him in vestures of fine linen, and put a gold chain about his neck; 43 And he made him to ride in the second chariot which he had; and they cried before him, Bow the knee: and he made him ruler over all the land of Egypt. 44 And Pharaoh said unto Joseph, I am Pharaoh, and without thee shall no man lift up his hand or foot in all the land of Egypt. 45 And Pharaoh called Joseph's name Zaphnathpaaneah; and he gave him to wife Asenath the daughter of Potipherah priest of On. And Joseph went out over all the land of Egypt.

This passage if full of the blessings that came with Joseph winning the battles of his life. At the end of all that he had to go through came the reward that he never expected came.

Take a look at this list of blessings:

1.   Pharaoh declares that none is wiser than Joseph

2. Pharaoh sets him over his house

3. Pharaoh declared that there shall be non-greater

4. My people shall be ruled according to your word

5. Only in matters of the throne will I be greater than you

6. Pharaoh set him over all the land of Egypt

7. Pharaoh dressed him in fine clothes

8. Put a gold chain around his neck

9. Put a ring on his finger

10. Made him ride in his second chariot

11. Everyone had to bow the knee

12. Pharaoh said to Joseph and without thee shall no man lift up his hand or foot in all the land of Egypt

13. He sent him throughout the land of Egypt

In addition to all of that Pharaoh gave him a wife now he no longer had to deal with loneliness or being alone, finally he can have a family again, but there was still something missing; he wanted to see his father and his brothers and for them to love him. Nothing was mentioned about this but anybody who has family that they love can say that they do not want to be abruptly separated and never know again if they are living or are dead. Still, he loves everyone as he always did.

Finally, the time has come for Joseph to get the desire of his heart, and that is to see his family again. Because of the famine that was over the land as described in Genesis 41:56-57.

Genesis 41:56-57

56 And the famine was over all the face of the earth: And Joseph opened all the storehouses, and sold unto the Egyptians; and the famine waxed sore in the land of Egypt. 57 And all countries came into Egypt to Joseph for to buy corn; because that the famine was so sore in all lands.

Joseph's family would have to come and buy corn and we can see what happened in Genesis 42:1-5.

Genesis 42:1-5

1 Now when Jacob saw that there was corn in Egypt, Jacob said unto his sons, Why do ye look one upon another? 2 And he said, Behold, I have heard that there is corn in Egypt: get you down thither, and buy for us from thence; that we may live, and not die. 3 And Joseph's ten brethren went down to buy corn in Egypt. 4 But Benjamin, Joseph's brother, Jacob sent not with his brethren; for he said, Lest peradventure mischief befall him. 5 And the sons of Israel came to buy corn among those that came: for the famine was in the land of Canaan.

Our God is amazing He knew all the time that Joseph would see his family again. Not only see them again but God wanted Joseph to feed them and then bring them into the land where He intended to grow the entire nation into a massive amount of people. When Joseph saw them he decided to test them, he had been through too much with them, he had loved them through all of this but he did not trust them. When Joseph saw them he recognized them but they did not recognize him. The account of this is found in Genesis chapter 42.

When the test was over Joseph revealed himself to his brothers. This is what happened in Genesis 45:1-4.

Genesis 45:1-4

1 Then Joseph could not refrain himself before all them that stood by him; and he cried, Cause every man to go out from me. And there stood no man with him, while Joseph made himself known unto his brethren. 2 And he wept aloud: and the Egyptians and the house of Pharaoh heard. 3 And Joseph said unto his brethren, I am Joseph; doth my father yet live? And his brethren could not answer him; for they were troubled at his presence. 4 And Joseph said unto his brethren, Come near to me, I pray you. And they came near. And he said, I am Joseph your brother, whom ye sold into Egypt.

This is even more amazing to me. Look what happened. Joseph was so happy to see his family he wept and he did not care who heard him. He loved them and to see them again was such a blessing to him. But their response was different. As we can see in Genesis 45:5-8.

Genesis 45:5-8

5 Now therefore be not grieved, nor angry with yourselves, that ye sold me hither: for God did send me before you to preserve life. 6 For these two years hath the famine been in the land: and yet there are five years, in the which there shall neither be earing nor harvest. 7 And God sent me before you to preserve you posterity in the earth, and to save your lives by a great deliverance. 8 So now it was not you that sent me hither, but God: and he hath made me a father to Pharaoh, and lord of all his house, and a ruler throughout all the land of Egypt.

His brothers were grieved and angry with themselves but Joseph continued to love them and told them that God had sent him to Egypt not them. How did Joseph know it was God and not them? It was because God was his only friend, he spent a tremendous amount of time with God and God helped him love as was required of him to be able to greet them all now in love. God wanted his family saved and they were because love never fails. If you have family members who seem to be unlovable or loveable and you want to win them to Christ start loving them unconditionally. Like Joseph, pay no attention to the evil done to you, if any and be longsuffering with them. These are some of the characteristics of love the Joseph employed to win the battle.

Joseph is now ready to do what God had intended for him to do when he gave him the dream. The only thing left is for him to do is to send for his father and all of the rest of him family members. Joseph explained to them what was happening with the famine and what he was going to do for them and then sent them back to get the rest of the family we see that in Genesis 45:9-15.

Genesis 45:9-15

9 Haste ye, and go up to my father, and say unto him, Thus saith thy son Joseph, God hath made me lord of all Egypt: come down unto me, tarry not: 10 And thou shalt dwell in the land of Goshen, and thou shalt be near unto me, thou, and thy children, and thy children's children, and thy flocks, and thy herds, and all that thou hast: 11 And there will I nourish thee; for yet there are five years of famine; lest thou, and thy household, and all that thou hast, come to poverty. 12 And, behold, your eyes see, and the eyes of my brother Benjamin, that it is my mouth that speaketh unto you. 13 And ye shall tell my father of all my glory in Egypt, and of all that ye have seen; and ye shall haste and bring down my father hither. 14 And he fell upon his brother Benjamin's neck, and wept; and Benjamin wept upon his neck. 15 Moreover he kissed all his brethren, and wept upon them: and after that his brethren talked with him.

This is a true testimony of the love of God, and when you tap into the love of God you tap into winning every time. Pharaoh's servants passed the news report of Joseph family to Pharaoh and it pleased Pharaoh and his servants, then in Genesis 45:17-18.

Genesis 45:17-18

17 And Pharaoh said unto Joseph, Say unto thy brethren, This do ye; lade your beasts, and go, get you unto the land of Canaan; 18 And take your father and your households, and come unto me: and I will give you the good of the land of Egypt, and ye shall eat the fat of the land.

Now Joseph has realized both of the dreams to have come to pass. His parents and his brothers had bowed down to him. Joseph did not get a big head about this, he reverend and honored God, and he was thankful that his family will be able to have good land and shall be able to eat the fat of the land at no cost to them, why because Joseph fought the battle of love and won. Joseph paid the price. In some respects he paid a price for them similar to some of the things that Jesus Christ paid for us because he loved us that much. Some of those characteristics of the price Joseph paid can be found in Isaiah 53:3-4.

Isaiah 53:3-4

3 He is despised and rejected of men; a man of sorrows, and acquainted with grief: and we hid as it were our faces from him; he was despised, and we esteemed him not. 4 Surely he hath borne our griefs, and carried our sorrows: yet we did esteem him stricken, smitten of God, and afflicted.

This passage is talking about the suffering that Jesus Christ would have to go through in order to save the world, but Joseph can identify with some of this because God gave him two dreams that told him from the beginning what his assignment was, he just did not know the process that he would have to complete before it manifested in the natural. Joseph was despised and rejected of men, he was a man of sorrows, he was acquainted with grief and all that he thought loved him hid their face from him, he carried all of that for them yet he was esteemed stricken and smitten of God and afflicted. Joseph was not physically beaten as Jesus was, nor did he have to die a physical death but he had to die to everything that was in him in opposite of love in order to love as he did. He had to die to pride, anger, hurt, rejection, insecurity, abandonment, being unwanted, unappreciated and unloved. All of those things were things that he had to reject and sometimes it seems on a daily basis, but it was worth it. He had to die to his flesh. He won the battle of his situations and circumstances with love.

Chapter 5 - Losing Battles

Those who tried to win their battles without love lost the battle big time. What can be so important that we would take a position to try to win without God, or try to override the word of God because of our situations or circumstances? That does not work. There is no in-between space when it comes to spiritual things.We are on the side of God or on the side of Satan. The example that I will use for this explanation is Cain, first born son of Adam and Eve after sin entered their lives. Since Cain was the firstborn he had opportunity to be the one that God would use to pass down the decedents to Jesus Christ. Choosing what you want for your life has to be one of the greatest events of your life because it is going to make the difference when it comes to where you will spend eternity, with or without God.

Cain – Over a process of time Cain brought an offering to the LORD, but the LORD was not pleased with his offering. His brother Abel also brought an offering to the LORD and the LORD was pleased with his offering. Then his brother Abel brought his offering to the Lord and the Lord has respect for Abel's offering. Cain had an attitude from the beginning. That is evident because he did not bring God his first as his brother Abel did in Genesis 4:4-5.

Genesis 4:4-5

4 And Abel, he also brought of the firstlings of his flock and of the fat thereof. And the LORD had respect unto Abel and to his offering. 5 But unto Cain and to his offering he had not respect. And Cain was very wroth, and his countenance fell.

Cain was very angry. The Hebrew word for wroth is charah which means to be hot, furious, burn, become angry, be kindled. God responded to Cain's anger and asked him why he was angry. Cain did not reply to the LORD. Rather, he continued to be prideful and angry not with God but with his brother. He did not love God or his brother. He wanted God to change His character to fit his situation. We do that sometimes, especially when we have been wounded, hurt, abused or misused. We want God to be upset with people because of their sin; God will never change His character to fit our circumstances or situations. We can see what God said to Cain in Genesis 4:6-7.

Genesis 4:6-7

6And the Lord said to Cain, Why are you angry? And why do you look sad and depressed and dejected? 7 If you do well, will you not be accepted? And if you do not do well, sin crouches at your door; its desire is for you, but you must master it.

Cain did not want to give up his unacceptable offering to the LORD. All he had to do was bring God another offering, but he refused to do that. Instead, he blamed his brother and thought that he could get rid of the requirement of an acceptable offering by getting rid of the one that brought the acceptable offering. That was envy. None of Cain's represented any characteristics of love, they were all the opposite of love. People who envy are different from those that are jealous because they do not want to do what they have to do to get what the person did to get what they got. In other words, Cain did not want to bring God an acceptable offering but he did not want his brother to have that honor either. Remember, his brother had done nothing to him, yet he wanted to destroy him.

It is very interesting what God told him. God gave him the answer to his situation but he did not want to love God or his brother he only wanted to love himself. He was self-seeking and insisting on his own way. He paid no attention to what God said to him. All he could think of was tricking his brother out into the field in order to kill him. That is even more interesting because some people actually think like Cain that they can get rid of people by taking them off the planet, but little do they know we are eternal beings and we are going to spend eternity with God or without Him in heaven with Him or hell without Him. Instead of taking the advice of God, Cain allowed sin to overtake him and he killed his brother. All of this is seen in Genesis 4:8.

Genesis 4:8

And Cain said to his brother, Let us go out to the field. And when they were in the field, Cain rose up against Abel his brother and killed him.

As a result, he lost the battle and the war. God had prepared a place for them in His presence, but Cain wanted his own way so badly that he gave all of that up. He lost the opportunity to be in God presence, he was exiled from his family, and now he has murder running rampant in his bloodline.

At the end of all that Cain did a death situation was penitently waiting. After he killed his brother see what God said to him in Genesis 4:10-12.

Genesis 4:10-12

And [the Lord] said, What have you done? The voice of your brother's blood is crying to Me from the ground. 11 And now you are cursed by reason of the earth, which has opened its mouth to receive your brother's [shed] blood from your hand. 12 When you till the ground, it shall no longer yield to you its strength; you shall be a fugitive and a vagabond on the earth [in perpetual exile, a degraded outcast].

What a price Cain had to pay. It was far worse than what he imagined. Notice the following list.

- He was cursed by reason of the earth
- The ground shall no longer yield to you
- You shall be a fugitive

- You shall be a vagabond
- You shall be in perpetual exile
- You are a degraded outcast

This is losing everything that he could possibly lose, but the greatest loss of all of these is losing the presence of God.

After Cain heard what God had to say, he was afraid of being killed, is not this interesting. He has just killed his brother but he does not want to be killed. Why? It was not him that put in his mind the idea to kill his brother, it was Satan. Do you know anybody that do things to other people that they cannot stand to happen to them? I do, It makes you wonder how they can be so comfortable doing hurtful and unhealthy things to others and can't stand for that very same thing to be done to them. You see how nobody likes for sin to fellowship with them, on the other hand everybody likes to be loved, when the love is real love.

When Cain mentioned to God that his punishment was too great, the LORD had mercy on him and set a mark on Cain. Take a look at what happened in Genesis 4:13-15.

Genesis 4:13-15

13 Then Cain said to the Lord, My punishment is [c]greater than I can bear. 14 Behold, You have driven me out this day from the face of the land, and from Your face I will be hidden; and I will be a fugitive and a vagabond and a wanderer on the earth, and whoever finds me will kill me. 15 And the Lord said to him,

*[d]Therefore, if anyone kills Cain, vengeance
shall be taken on him sevenfold. And the Lord
set a [e]mark or sign upon Cain, lest anyone
finding him should kill him. AMP*

Cain finally understood what he had to give up. He
realized that he could no longer blame his brother and
now he tells God "you have driven me out from the face
of the land and from your face. Cain also realized that he
had to leave the presence of his family and the presence
of God. He would no longer be able to enjoy the access
that he once had with his mother and father or God. He
had to leave everything and everyone that he loved. Once
his conversation with God was over he left as stated in
Genesis 4:16.

Genesis 4:16

*So Cain went away from the presence of the
Lord and dwelt in the land of Nod [wandering],
east of Eden. AMP*

This was not the worst of it. I can imagine that Cain was
thinking like many of us that his sin would not affect
anyone but him, however this was not true. Cain passed
that desire to murder down through his bloodline. We see
what happened with his decedent in Genesis 4:23-24.

Genesis 4:23-24

*Lamech said to his wives, Adah and Zillah, Hear
my voice; you wives of Lamech, listen to what I
say; for I have slain a man [merely] for*

wounding me, and a young man [only] for striking and bruising me. 24 If Cain is avenged sevenfold, truly Lamech [will be avenged] seventy-sevenfold. AMP

Lamech was 4 generations from Cain and look at what he said. He killed two men and based on Cain's example he will be avenged seventy-sevenfold even though Cain was only avenged sevenfold. What a witness and a testimony of losing big time. Lamech did not know that he had missed the opportunity to be in the presence of God just because his great, great, great, grandfather Cain would not submit to the word of God, he wanted to hold on to his pride and he did.

There are many others but I choose Cain because his choices allowed us to follow his bloodline down through history. He was the head of the group that did not follow the leading of God so they were not a part of establishing the spiritual history that Seth bloodline established. If you follow the linage of Cain you will be able to see some of the things that they established in the following passage in Genesis 4:16-17.

Genesis 4:16-17

And Cain went out from the presence of the LORD, and dwelt in the land of Nod, on the east of Eden. 17 And Cain knew his wife; and she conceived, and bare Enoch: and he builded a city, and called the name of the city, after the name of his son, Enoch.

We can see that Cain was doing some things, he built a city but it was not built on the foundation of God. This direction that Cain had chosen kept getting worse with each generation. Cain did something else that his father Adam did not teach him and that was having many wives. Adam had only one wife, Cain introduced multiple wives and some people are still struggling with that today.

Cain was introducing all that he did into the earth and teaching that to his decedents. Now we have the multiple wife idea traveling down through generations. This is found in Genesis 4:18-19.

Genesis 4:18-19 18

And unto Enoch was born Irad: and Irad begat Mehujael: and Mehujael begat Methusael: and Methusael begat Lamech. 19 And Lamech took unto him two wives: the name of the one was Adah, and the name of the other Zillah.

We know that God does not want His people to marry more than one wife. God has made it clear that He does not want His leaders to lead the people incorrectly in this matter. He gave Moses instructions to give to the people describing what he required of kings and their descendants if they wanted to live alone in that position. We can see that in Deuteronomy 17:15-20.

Deuteronomy 17:15-20

15 Thou shalt in any wise set him king over thee, whom the LORD thy God shall choose: one from among thy brethren shalt thou set king over thee: thou mayest not set a stranger over thee, which is not thy brother. 16 But he shall not multiply horses to himself, nor cause the people to return to Egypt, to the end that he should multiply horses: forasmuch as the LORD hath said unto you, Ye shall henceforth return no more that way. 17 Neither shall he multiply wives to himself, that his heart turn not away: neither shall he greatly multiply to himself silver and gold. 18 And it shall be, when he sitteth upon the throne of his kingdom, that he shall write him a copy of this law in a book out of that which is before the priests the Levites: 19 And it shall be with him, and he shall read therein all the days of his life: that he may learn to fear the LORD his God, to keep all the words of this law and these statutes, to do them: 20 That his heart be not lifted up above his brethren, and that he turn not aside from the commandment, to the right hand, or to the left: to the end that he may prolong his days in his kingdom, he, and his children, in the midst of Israel.

If seems like Cain was prospering, he was, but in the wrong direction. It was making inroads in the things of the world systems that Satan control, which he got from Adam. If we understand what the world systems are we can also understand what was happening. The world systems are the kingdoms of this world. They are sometimes called seven mountains:

1. Business
2. Government
3. Media
4. Arts and Entertainment
5. Education
6. Family
7. Religion

Now we can more readily identify what was happening in world history from the lineage of Cain. God's people are encouraged to keep His commandments, but the world systems ignore God's commandments. Cain was conducting business but not God's way, he was educating people but not God's way, he was raising up families but not God's way, he was sending our media messages but not God's way, he was creating arts and entertainment but not God's way and his religion was centered around him. Let's take a look at some of these. Some of his descendants raised cattle, these were business men in Genesis 4:20.

Genesis 4:20

And Adah bare Jabal: he was the father of such as dwell in tents, and of such as have cattle.

Some created instruments for arts and entrainment as seen in Genesis 4:21.

Genesis 4:12

And his brother's name was Jubal: he was the father of all such as handle the harp and organ.
We know that there was probably no music coming from these instruments that were worshiping God. Some were craftsmen in brass and iron, more business in Genesis 4:22.

Genesis 4:22

And Zillah, she also bare Tubalcain, an instructer of every artificer in brass and iron: and the sister of Tubalcain was Naamah.

Satan uses whoever will allow him to influence people to follow his way and many don't even realize that Satan is behind what they are doing. God has dealt with that in Revelation 11:15.

Revelation 11:15

And the seventh angel sounded; and there were great voices in heaven, saying, The kingdoms of this world are become the kingdoms of our Lord, and of his Christ; and he shall reign for ever and ever.

Those that are believers who are assigned to one of these kingdoms now have dominion over that particular kingdom. They will have to use the love factor in order to do whatever they do. There is no love lost or gained from the generations of Cain because it is not even a consideration for any of them.

Now if you follow world history and bible history timelines you will notice that the descendants of Cain were making history in the world systems while God's people were leaving the information that God wanted people to have to stay connected with Him. If you notice the IronAge and the BronzeAge other things were going on in world history time periods were recorded from the exploits of the generations of Cain, but the history that was made by the bloodline of Seth is recorded in the bible as instructions for life from the word of God.

What a price Cain paid, to be separated from God forever is not worth, land, houses, tents, position, cities, arts and entrainment, education, government, family control, business, media, education or anything at all. Satan cannot promise you anything but eternity with him in hell. He does not present it that way to people, but all of the success and progress that was made here on earth is not eternal, you can't take any of that with you when you leave the planet it all has to stay behind. How many of these things do the people of God love more than God? We have to understand that God knew that He wanted us to love each other but we should with our brothers. He wanted that to be a lifestyle for us as Jesus had said in John 15:12.

John 15:12

This is my commandment, That ye love one another, as I have loved you.

This is not an option it is a command. When we practice love as a lifestyle, these things seem so unimportant in the scheme of things.

Chapter 6 – Positioning To Win Battles

The first part of understanding the importance of applying love to ever battle is to realize that no matter what we do or say nothing will position us to win except love. We must be in a position to win. We can if we choose position ourselves to lose. Positioning ourselves to get things done is not a strange concept to us. It is just like filling out applications and forms, for example, when we start any kind of school at any age level we must apply or fill out forms, that act is positioning yourself to get what you are trying to get done. We have to position ourselves to do anything. If we want to take a trip we must position ourselves by purchasing a ticket for transportation or get a vehicle ready that we plan to drive etc. Losing is not an option for those who understand the principle of love. We must first consider what battles are and understand that we go into some kind of battle every day of our lives.

Battles are not just physically or verbally fighting. The definition of battle covers many areas of our lives that we have not considered battles. A battle is a hostile encounter with another person, or group of people but it is also an encounter to fight against or for something (a cause, freedom, court trials, and beliefs). The battle is also tangible and useful in fighting for social and professional positions, job security, health issues, getting rid of sickness, political campaigns, successful living, any person, place or things that could be considered an enemy or any situations that you desire to change to make better or get rid of worse cases just to name a few.

The Dictionary.com definition of battle: 1. A hostile encounter or engagement between opposing military forces: the battle of Waterloo. 2. Participation in such hostile encounters or engagements: wounds received in battle. 3. A fight between two persons or animals: ordering a trial by battle to settle the dispute. 4. Any conflict or struggle: a battle for control of the Senate. 5. To engage in battle: ready to battle with the enemy. 6. To work very hard or struggle; strive: to battle for freedom. 7. To fight (a person, army, cause, etc.): We battled strong winds and heavy rains in our small boat. 8. To force or accomplish by fighting, struggling, etc.: He battled his way to the top of his profession. 9. Give / do battle, to enter into conflict; fight: He was ready to do battle for his beliefs. 10. Synonyms: 1. Contest, conflict, war. Battle, action, skirmish mean a conflict between organized armed forces.

A battle is a prolonged and general conflict pursued to a definite decision: the **Battle of the Bulge in World War II**. A skirmish is a slight engagement, often on the periphery of an area of battle: several minor skirmishes. An action can be a battle or a skirmish or can refer to actual fighting or combat: a major military action; action along the border; He saw action in the campaign, 2. Conflict 3, Contest, 4. Contention; struggle: his battle for recognition, 5. do battle, give battle, join to start fighting, 6. To fight in or as if in military combat; contend (with): she battled against cancer, 7. to struggle in order to achieve something or arrive somewhere: he battled through the crowd or 8. To scrape a living, especially by doing odd jobs etc. It is important to understand that no matter what you do or say, no matter how much you sacrifice no matter how you apply knowledge and experience to situations, no matter how eloquently you can speak, no matter how much you can understand difficult things and no matter how much you personally accomplish you cannot win without the attributes of love. If you try to fight the battle without love you are just making noise, you will not be in a position of influence nor will any of those things assist you, be of any use, or be advantageous or profitable in your efforts to win the battle.

Many times we will say to ourselves "I have done all we know to do" but there is one things lacking we have not applied love to all of the efforts that we brought forth to this point.

When you do not understand how to apply love or that you should employ love to work on your behalf burdens, yokes, arguments, strife, disappointments, rejections and misunderstanding, to name a few are formed. How do you employ love on your behalf? Follow the following directions below, because these actions are actions of LOVE.

1. The first thing you have to do is to humble yourself to a position of apparent loss. By that I mean always give the other person the upper hand. To employ love in this area you have to be completely patient (some people say that they have patience but they have a short fuse, that is not patience, that is partly patient,

not completely patience), not to lose heart because of the trouble that is at hand, persevere patiently and bravely in enduring misfortunes and troubles, be patient in bearing the offenses and injuries of others, be mild and slow in avenging, be longsuffering with them, be slow to anger, and be slow to punish for mistakes and errors. One thing that I have noticed from talking to a few people working for a company or corporation is that they are now charging money to people who make mistakes. Many times mistakes cost the company money but something must happen in the process of learning or training for the position. Other companies fire people for their first mistake. That may or may not be an injustice but it is definitely a seed that impact future battles. Following the instructions of love may seem to be doing things to your own hurt but this is the power of love and it is working for your good and not for your hurt. You say how is this working for my good?Well let's take a look at a few of these. What kind of response do you get when you respond with anger? Usually a heated confrontation that all parties regret and nothing is accomplished but the fruit of unhappy or undesired results. Also, if you are offended or emotionally injured (broken hearted) you tend to want to quit, run, hide or give up the process all of which causes you to leave the battle and lose by default.

2. Be kind; use kindness as a matter of course in all your dealings with people because there is no unkind response to an act of kindness. Do not boil with envy thus desiring what someone else has causing a

feeling of discontentment or resentful longing for and aroused by someone else's possessions, qualities, achievements or stature. These resentful emotions are based on perceptions that what the other person has is better and it will also cause you to wish that the other lacked it. What a waste of time incorrect perceptions often accompany a lack of understanding or misunderstanding. Your opinion of what they have has nothing to do with what you want. You must stay focused and reject the negative energy that these kinds of activities bring.

3. You must not be jealous fearing the loss of someone or something that is attached to or possess by you or another person. If that thing or person (not a spouse) wants to leave it is for your good you may be far better off without that person. Do not be jealous, afraid of losing what should be gone from your life nor of what belongs to some else anyway. Sometimes people who do not celebrate you are the ones that you want to win over or keep in your life, but you must let those go because if they do not celebrate you and if they stay close to you there a hindrance that is hidden from you because of their nonsupport of your vision overtly or covertly.

4. Do not boast one's self or self-display, employing rhetorical embellishments in extolling one's self excessively. Do not be puffed up or boastful and make yourself more important than you really are, thus showing excessive self-esteem. This is an act of rudeness and arrogance.

5. Do not be out of order according to accepted standards of good behavior and good taste nor act in an inappropriate manner according to the circumstances presented at the moment.

6. Do not insist on your own rights or your own way, for love is not self-seeking; it is not touchy or fretful or resentful; it takes no account of the evil done to it nor does love pay any attention to a suffered wrong.

7. Do not rejoice at injustice and unrighteousness, but rejoices when things are right and when truth triumphs.

8. Do not be afraid of anything or anybody that come along because there is no fear in love; but perfect love cast out fear because fear has torment.Aperson that does not fear is mature in love because they are able to tolerate anything and everything that shows up, and is ready to believe the best of every person, their hopes are fadeless under all circumstances and conditions, and they are able to withstand everything without wearying.

Love Never Fails

1 Corinthians 13:8-9

Love never fails [never fades out or becomes obsolete or comes to an end]. As for prophecy ([d]the gift of interpreting the divine will and purpose), it will be fulfilled and pass away; as for tongues, they will be destroyed and cease; as for knowledge, it will pass away [it will lose its value and be superseded by truth]. 9 For our knowledge is fragmentary (incomplete and imperfect), and our prophecy (our teaching) is fragmentary (incomplete and imperfect). AMP

You cannot win battles with brute force alone. History has proven that with the many wars locally, nationally, internationally and world wars. You must have battle strategies, good or bad weather depending on the strategy and good or bad physical surroundings depending on your battle plan. In addition your motives for fighting must be based on love exemplifying the characteristics that demonstrate love.

WorldWar II was the last world war and that was one of the most devastating because the war initiators started the war not just to win additional territory or minerals like coal, precious metals like silver or gold but also to destroy a nation of people that had done nothing to warrant. The last major battle of that war was called the "Battle of the Bulge" it is historically one of America's greatest battles; however, it is significant because it freed the nation of people that were targeted for destruction. It is not my intention to talk about wars but I do want to say initiating battles with motives of intolerance, impatience, hot headedness, hot tempers, anger, self-exaltations, meanness, envy, jealousy, injustice or just for the sake of avoiding the truth will inevitably lead you to a loss and your efforts will fail. These attitudes are the basis that you can use to position yourself to lose the battle. Building a gallows to hang people, corporations, organizations etc. just because of dislike, envy or jealously may cause you to end up on the gallows that you build. A great example of that is Haman, and by the way he was trying to destroy the same nation of people that Adolf Hitler was trying to destroy in World War II. Haman hated one person because he would not bow down to him and because of that he purposed to kill him and the whole nation of people that he belonged to. His wife gave him the idea of the avenue to kill Mordecai in Esther 5:14.

Esther 5:14

Then said Zeresh his wife and all his friends unto him, Let a gallows be made of fifty cubits high, and to morrow speak thou unto the king that Mordecai may be hanged thereon: then go thou in merrily with the king unto the banquet. And the thing pleased Haman; and he caused the gallows to be made.

Haman liked the idea and went immediately to the king to get permission in Esther 6:4.

Esther 6:4
And the king said, Who is in the court? Now Haman was come into the outward court of the king's house, to speak unto the king to hang Mordecai on the gallows that he had prepared for him.

Everything that Haman setup forMordechai backfired on him, he had to honor Mordecai when he had planned to dishonor and kill him. When Haman was positive that the

king wanted to honor him, it was Mordecai that the king
wanted to honor.

Esther 6:3-11

*11 And the king said, What honour and dignity
hath been done to Mordecai for this? Then said
the king's servants that ministered unto him,
There is nothing done for him. 4 And the king
said, Who is in the court? Now Haman was
come into the outward court of the king's house,
to speak unto the king to hang Mordecai on the
gallows that he had prepared for him. 5 And the
king's servants said unto him, Behold, Haman
standeth in the court. And the king said, Let him
come in. 6 So Haman came in. And the king said
unto him, What shall be done unto the man
whom the king delighteth to honour? Now
Haman thought in his heart, To whom would the
king delight to do honour more than to myself?
7 And Haman answered the king, For the man
whom the king delighteth to honour, 8 Let the
royal apparel be brought which the king useth to
wear, and the horse that the king rideth upon,
and the crown royal which is set upon his head:
9 And let this apparel and horse be delivered to
the hand of one of the king's most noble princes,
that they may array the man withal whom the
king delighteth to honour, and bring him on
horseback through the street of the city, and
proclaim before him, Thus shall it be done to the
man whom the king delighteth to honour. 10
Then the king said to Haman, Make haste, and*

take the apparel and the horse, as thou hast said, and do even so to Mordecai the Jew, that sitteth at the king's gate: let nothing fail of all that thou hast spoken. 11 Then took Haman the apparel and the horse, and arrayed Mordecai, and brought him on horseback through the street of the city, and proclaimed before him, Thus shall it be done unto the man whom the king delighteth to honour.

And finally Haman was hung on the same gallows that he had built to hang Mordecai.

Esther 7:9-10

And Harbonah, one of the chamberlains, said before the king, Behold also, the gallows fifty cubits high, which Haman had made for Mordecai, who had spoken good for the king, standeth in the house of Haman. Then the king said, Hang him thereon. 10 So they hanged Haman on the gallows that he had prepared for Mordecai. Then was the king's wrath pacified.

Haman lost the battle big time. His choices affected his family as well. They too lost because husband and father did not want to walk in love.

Chapter 7 – Choose Your Battles

Many times we win a few battles but lose the war or we may win the war and then find out that we really did not want the results of that particular victory. Have you ever purchased something you thought you really wanted and then when you got home you had second thoughts, or have you ever wanted to go to see a particular movie that you thought that you would really like or have you ever gone to an amusement park expecting something different than you found there.

We must choose our battles wisely for many times we waste time and energy just because we want to always be right. It may be wise to choose and strategize a battle to prepare and position yourself to increase your income but not to battle with your neighbor about their tree leaves blowing in your yard. It may be wise to battle with bad habits you want to get rid of or to improve your health by losing weight but not wise to battle for a position in an organization that you really don't want but you don't want the person that may get it to have it. Take your time and think about what you are about to take on and ask yourself is this really worth the fight.

The battle must be for something big enough for the outcome to be significant to you or your family. Why waste time money and energy to do something to gain $20.00 when the total cost of the battle was $1000.00.

Recognize that all of your life issues battles of big and small issues.

Sometimes the fight does more harm than good and you may not get the desired results especially when you go to battle for your personal rights. Make sure you want the results of the victory more than the excitement of the battle. Remember if you go to battle and fight about everything no one will take you seriously.

It is possible to love the fight out of people or situations. Try smiling at an angry person and telling them that you love them, they will do one of two things: 1. Tell you that you need to stop playing, (because they are serious about this fight) or smile back. What is their response? Usually they will say "stop joking around" because they find it hard to believe that you are expressing love to them at the same time that they are giving you some sharp words verbally, especially if they do not understand that love is a weapon and it is more serious and effective than anger. If one of the persons in the middle of a heated conversation would just stop arguing and switch to the proven characteristics of love they will find that the whole confrontations will lose steam and cool down to something less than smoldering ashes.

Have you ever tried to stop a heated confrontation with more heated conversation, separation of the parties involved or some other traditional method? If you have then you know that it takes a while for that to happen and sometimes it does not happen at all the confrontation escalates to a physical fight. However if you apply love as explained earlier in whatever area is appropriate at the moment you will find that works quickly and it never fails. Let me caution you though, if you wait until you are in the middle of a battle to use the characteristics of love it will be too late. You must practice every day starting with what you can handle at the moment and allow yourself to mature into more and more of the characteristics until your character engages love automatically without you having to think about what you are saying or doing.

I have tried to stop all kinds of battles of confrontations physical, psychological, emotional and conversational with words of wisdom, knowledge and reason and it just did not work at all. Eventually the parties calmed down but that was never the end of it. But when I learned to approach each situation with love the matter was settled quickly and completely. You may know someone that will turn down being loved but I have never seen anyone turn down love.

Love works in all situations, I remember on one occasion I was attending a fashion show and it was at the time I had just begin to learn how to love people and I begin to practice loving the participants of the fashion show. I smile each time they walked down the runway and I had purposed in my heart that I would let them know what a good job they were doing by just loving them in my heart. The participants were male and female and when they looked in my face they could not help but smile and found it very difficult to focus on what they were supposed to be doing and that is when I begin to learn the true power of love. I had never seen any of them prior to that event and I never spoke to any after the show nor have I seen any of them since that time but I know that they know that I loved them. I am sure they were wondering who I was or if they knew me because there should have not been any reason for a perfect stranger to love them.

On another occasion two people were having a heated conversation based on what they were talking about they were both missing the point and I was able to separate them without pushing, shelving, or any other physical method, I used the characteristic of love to talk to one that calmed them down long enough for me to get to the other one and calm them down without condemning, complaining, finger pointing or trying to insert anything in except love they both enjoyed being loved. As I begin to love both of them peace found its way into their hearts. That was something they could have done for themselves if they only knew to win.We cannot win fighting each other; we must love each other in order to win. If we must fight it should be evil. We fight the Devil; we do not fight a person (flesh and blood) that is God's word about how to handle that.

Nobody turns down love, people want to be loved. It is so valuable because there is no way to get it unless it is given freely to you. You can't buy it. Have you ever known people that do all kinds of things to get people to love them, or to get attention paid to them? I have seen all kind of things that people do to try to make people love them. That cannot be done, you cannot purchase love, you cannot bargain with people to get them to love you or work for it. Love is a choice; people have to choose to love you or they can choose not to love

you.What you do have control over is to love them with
the help of the Holy Spirit. There are examples of people
in the bible of people trying to get people to love them
and were never able to make that happen. Sampson
wanted Delilah to love him but that never happened, he
is going back to her over and over and was willing to risk
losing his strength, the God given gift that he was to use
as a judge of Israel.All she wanted to know was the
source of his strength, she did not love him nor did she
choose to we see in Judges 16:6.

Judges 16:6

**And Delilah said to Samson, Tell me, I pray
thee, wherein thy great strength lieth, and
wherewith thou mightest be bound to afflict thee.**

He wanted her to love him, therefore he kept going back
until he eventually did lose his strength but was never
able to get her to love him. Another example is that of
Leah trying to get Jacob to love her, but he never choose
to do so, we see that in Genesis 29:32.

Genesis 29:32

**And Leah conceived, and bare a son, and she
called his name Reuben: for she said, Surely the
LORD hath looked upon my affliction; now
therefore my husband will love me.**

She bore more son for him than any of his wives
including the one that he did love, but Leah was never
able to do anything to get him to love her. God wants us
to love people because we choose to do so, that is how

He does it, He loves us because He chooses to not because we have done anything to deserve it. Our direction from God is to choose to love people. We are commanded to love regardless of what they do to us. God did not give us any excuse that we could use not to love. In fact He said not to owe anybody anything but love in Romans 13:8.

Romans 13:8

owe no man anything, but to love one another: for he that loveth another hath fulfilled the law.

If the law is fulfilled when you love then you are going to win when you practice loving people.

Chapter 8 – Practical Characteristics of Love

Love works all the time and it never fails. If you were to go down the list of characteristics of love I believe that you will find out that you have been doing some of these and did not even know it. For instance, as a child growing up do you remember any of your care givers (parents, grand-parents, child care etc.) ever taking something from you that you did not want to give up? If you do, you remember that you did not like that at all. However, most of the time they were things that would harm a child that was too young to be able to use it properly, but for whatever the reason we felt a sense of loss. One thing is for sure losing is not a pleasant experience. That is why it is difficult to give up things even if we don't want them. You had to give the care giver the upper hand because they insisted but when you yield to someone else backing out of a heated battle you actually position yourself to win. Whenever you are forced to do something you have already lost but when you back up deliberately you are in control of your actions and you win. That is one of the characteristics of love – letting the other person have what appears to be the upper hand when they are clearly wrong. Love will fix that immediately because they will say to you "you knew that you were wrong in the first place" and think that they won but later on when they have time to think about it they come back to you and apologize for their bad behavior or at least admit that they were wrong. Now see how easy it is to employ love on your behalf and let love win the battle for you.

How about kindness, this characteristic of love is special because it gives helpfulness to others that may or may not deserve it especially when a hot headed person demands an answer from you when you employ the kindness of love and give a kind response with a soft answer it turns away wrath, but grievous words stir up anger and anger causes strife and strife causes you to lose the battle. Have you ever noticed how long the results of anger stay in your thought process especially if you feel that you have been violated in some way? Your time is too valuable to spend it thinking about a lost battle. It is so much quicker and more pleasant to employ the kindness of love to fight the battle and settle the issue turning away wrath and moving on to your next agenda item with no more thought or concern of this event.

These next two envy and jealously are very subtle and they are also show stoppers because they hide from view. They hide because they know that if you ever find out what love knows about you that will be a great incentive to kick them to the curb. You cannot trust envy or jealously to tell you the truth because they do not know your truth they only acknowledge the truth of others. You cannot live by the truth of others you must live by your own truth. That is why we have to trust and employ love to go to bat for you because love knows something about you that envy and jealously do not. Love knows that you are wonderfully and beautifully made. Loves know that you have gifts and talents that are very important and nobody can do them as well and you can. Love knows that you are very special and unique and without you many will miss what you bring to the table and it is usually something the fits their needs. However, envy and jealousy can only see good things in other people and never has anything good to say about you and that is because they just don't know that is why you can never employ them to fight for you.

The best position for envy and jealously is in the unemployment line because they will not work for the one that pays them, they will only work for the one that is not giving them a dime because they want you to go after something that you have not paid for and that will cause you to lose the battle. What do I mean by that? Every life lesson that you have learned, you paid for in time and effort and no one can take that from you. All of your intellect and education that you have acquired over the years belongs to you. You paid for that with patience, perseverance and long hours of study, reading, writing and giving up fun and play time. No one can take that from you. All of your likes and dislikes belong to you, your taste buds, desires and habits, good or bad belong to you and you paid for that with selection by your choice of what is good or not good to you and for you. Not one person can take that from you.

There are some areas in your life that you have obtained favor from people, business or corporations because of your willingness to make the sacrifices needed to be made that cause them to want to favor you. You paid the price for that and it cannot be taken from you nor is it available to those who did not make the same sacrifices for whatever reason. If that is true for you and it is then it is also true for other people and what they paid for cannot be taken by anyone. However, envy and jealously hides this fact from people and try to convince them that they can get something that they did not pay for or qualify for something that they did not pay for. There are some things that you know if people do that thing hoping for a particular result they are not going to get what they expect because you have already paid the price and you know the truth of it. That can be shared with others but it cannot be taken from you. I remember some years back when I was working with a group of people in corporate America they wanted to try particular methods to solve a problem. I have spent much time and money trying that same method and I knew that it was not going to work but they wanted to do it anyway because they thought that they could do what I could not. I was not intimidated because I knew that method was not going to solve that problem. They were able to get management support that I was not able to get, they were able to get more money than I was able to get approved and that could have been a time of jealously or envy but what I knew could not be taken from me even if they did not believe me so I just sat back and waited and sure enough they got the same results that I have come to know several years before. It took them a long time to come to the conclusion that I started with. I am so glad that I had passed the stage of getting jealous and angry with folks as I had done in the past because I employed envy and jealously instead of love. I was content and went on to my next assignment without another thought of what they were doing or not doing. Employ love to work on your behalf and get rid of envy and jealously and win the battle because neither you nor I have time to be angry and discontented.

Rudeness and Arrogance are two other characteristics that love avoids. It is really interesting to me of how love lets you know what not to do. Love understands the return of the investment in rudeness and arrogance. While love encourages you to think well of yourself it also lets us know that we must not have a big head and think more of ourselves than we should. Have you ever talked to someone whose conversation is all about them and they see themselves as the best and the greatest in everything. That usually translates into rudeness and arrogance.

Rudeness is described in Merriam-Webster Dictionary with the following words: discourteousness, disrespect, impertinence, impoliteness, impudence, incivility, inconsiderateness, insolence, discourtesy or ungraciousness and these are just a few. I know that you need some examples because most of the time people use the word rude but they do not say what was actually done. One example is unsolicited interruptions into conversations of other people. When people do that they are saying their ideas, thoughts, needs, concerns and time are more important than any of the people already engaged in conversation and whatever they are talking about can wait until they all take care of your issue, in addition they have absolutely no interest in participating in what is being said. You may have better examples but the ones that I hear the most are as follows: leaving ice trays empty, not cleaning up after yourself, being consistently late for appointments, deliberately being noisy and listening to private conversations, reading mail not addressed to you, not addressing people when you enter a room with some kind of greeting or borrowing something without permission and believing that is acceptable. Rudeness and Arrogance are both subject to cultural and environment caveats.

Arrogance on the other hand is described by Merriam-Webster Dictionary as an attitude of superiority manifested in an overbearing manner or in presumptuous claims or assumptions of oneself and that is describes with the following words: assumption, conceitedness, consequence, haughtiness, hauteur, high horse, huffiness, bossiness, loftiness, lordliness, masterfulness, peremptoriness, pomposity, snobbishness, audacity, pretense, pretension, pretentiousness, self-consequence, self-importance, scorn and superiority. People who exhibit these characteristics are usually people who think that they are better than everybody else. They always want the conversations focused on them, they like to blow their own horn, showcasing their accomplishments, abilities etc. and if the subject changes they get offended or irritated.

Love understands the consequences of Rudeness and Arrogance (no regard for others) and when you have no regard for others they will disrespect or dishonor your request thus you lose the battle. So next time you have the opportunity to be rude or arrogant drop it like a hot potato and employ love and love will cause people to blow your horn for you instead of you having to do it yourself so that you can win in this arena every time.

Another thing that love will not do is act in an inappropriate manner. Appropriate behavior can usually be defined by social and cultural norms but they are common in certain aspects for instance, violence that is not self-defense against someone for personal gain, unwanted or unsolicited sexual advances, breathing down someone's neck when they are trying to work, leaving shopping carts in parking spaces rather than designated areas, yelling and screaming at people, acts of injustice or things similar to that kind of behavior. There are rules and regulations for any and everything in a given society. There are rules you should follow when you visit someone's home. You cannot go into someone's home and set your own rules, you have no authority there and that is an inappropriate behavior. Not all of the time, but most of the time inappropriate behavior has to do with actions of breaking rules, anger, offense or arrogance. For instance, some people will live out their frustrations by throwing things, knocking a hole in a wall, hit someone, kick someone, knock down a door, break car windows, let air out of tires, eating someone else's lunch that was stored in the corporate refrigerator without asking etc.

Love will not participate in any of those kinds of actions because the results of these kinds of actions always result in a response something negative and you cannot win with negative energy floating around. Rules are set in place for those who will to break that for whatever reason. They are not there for people who will honor rules. They do not need the rule because they act appropriately without having a rule shown in their face. Have you ever noticed the key locks that some companies use to put on file cabinets? That always amazed me because the reason for the locks were always founded to the protection from thieves, robbers, corporate spies etc., but if you know anything about those kind of folks, they have the tools to snap those locks of in a matter of seconds, so why the locks, they were for noisy people that would get the information and act inappropriately with it. If you are one of the persons that needed access to the information they would give you a key but if you did not need access they should have been able to trust you not to go in the file cabinet. The same way you would not expect someone to come into your home and go into your refrigerator, pantry, or bedroom closets without permission. That is a violation of your property and authority.

Love understands order and appropriateness and if you follow the example of love you can win in small, medium and large arenas because inappropriate behavior is never appropriate and almost never tolerated. Start out with winning in mind and be a part of solutions not problems.

How about having a hot temper? Love does not approve of hot temper characteristics. According to the Dictionary.com, hot tempered people can be described as bad-humored, bearish, unreasonable, crabby, cross, crotchety, annoying, disagreeable, got up on wrong side of bed, grouchy, grumpy, impatient , illhumored, irascible, irritable, like a bear, mean, ornery, out of sorts, perverse, quick-tempered, ratty, snappish, argumentative, ugly, and unpleasant. How does love handle that? No hot tempered persons consider themselves practicing these associated characteristics. If you say to a hot tempered person in the middle of a temper blow out "stop being so grouchy etc." they will usually say "I am not grouchy" in a grouch way. That is because they don't see themselves as that, grumpy,mean, impatient or an ornery person. There is not a time when one of the hot tempered attitudes will be able to win a battle when the result of the battle is seeking peaceful solutions, favorable understandings, satisfactory agreement or mutual settlements. Love understands that completely and endeavors to position to win battles. To that end, love does not approve of hot tempered characteristics and encourage us to calm down quickly. When you are engaged in these types of characteristics, the decisions you make are usually regrettable because you don't have time to think about what you should do or say, you just react and whatever comes to your mind you do that.And during that process of not thinking, select the activities that you think will solve the problem, deal with the situation in other words win the battle are always harmful more often than not cause you to lose the battle.

Another characteristic of love is not rejoicing in evil if you want to use the love strategy to win battles. You must not rejoice when wicked, unjust and unrighteousness things happen. Dictionary.Com describes wicked as evil or morally bad in principle or practice; sinful; iniquitous: wicked people; wicked habits. It comes from the word wick which means a bundle or loose twist or braid of soft threads, or a woven strip or tube, as of cotton or asbestos, which in a candle, lamp, oil stove, or the like, serves to draw up the melted tallow or wax or the oil or other flammable liquid to be burned. The important thing to note here is that wicks are twisted and when you take a close look at this characteristic you can see that it involves twisted thinking. Many times when people engage in these kinds of activities they like to do them in the dark so that they will not be caught but everything but love knows that everything that is done in the dark will come to the light, and when it comes to the light it is usually a painful process. It causes trust issues with the person or people involved and even though forgiveness is granted there is waiting and proving time to regain trust, therefore love wants us to save time and energy and make sure that everything we do is done in the light. Love does not want us to rejoice when we witness or participate in unrighteousness because love want you to rejoice when things are right and when truth triumphs.

Sometimes people are in the midst of trying to make something happen for them and they find themselves also in the midst of these kinds of situations and sometimes it is by no fault of their own they begin to be glad and rejoice when the see something bad happening to whoever or whatever. Take note of one example. Many times people celebrate these kinds of things when they want to get someone back for some infringement that was done to them by a particular person, business, corporation, institution, etc. They truly want to get them back for that particular violation. It may not be an individual violation; it may be corporate as in families, or other groups of people they are attached to so when they hear of or see something bad happening they rejoice and are really happy about their misfortunes.

This brings to mind the time I needed to ship some very valuable china and crystal from the west coast to the east coast. I called a particular company and ask them how to ship and how to insure the items. These were heirlooms that were passed down to me and I wanted to pass through our family for generations to come. The company gave me the instructions on how to pack the boxes and the price for shipping and the insurance. I packed the items according to the directions they had given me and shipped them. When they arrived on the east coast most of them were broken into small pieces. Some of the items were antique and I could not replace them even for money. I was expecting them to at least give the $10,000.00 insurance coverage which was nowhere near the cost to replace the items. I called them and they refused to honor the insurance they insisted that it was my fault because I should have packed it better, even though I packed the boxes according to their instructions in additions to not honoring an insurance claim that I paid for some of the persons I spoke to were rude and short tempered with me.

The crystal and china was crushed like crushed ice. I was hurt and angry. I could not believe that they would go to that much effort to cheat me and not pay me when the damage was clearly their fault. I could not believe that they would not honor an insurance claim that I paid for in order to have protection from damage of the items. I did not practice love on them in the beginning, I complained, I criticized and whatever else I could think of at the time, however over time I realized I did not want that to happen to anyone and I especially did not want to conduct business that way with my customers.

I should have been kind and forgiving in the beginning and that would have given them opportunity to show me favor and pay me for my loss but I just wanted them to suffer for my loss. Eventually I forgave them and went on, shortly after that I was doing business with another company that told me that they were canceling their contract with this shipper after twenty four years and I realized what a financial loss that was for the shipper. I did not mention what had happen to me at their hand but when it first happened love was the last thing on my mind, I was very angry and wanted some kind of satisfaction for my loss. But once I recovered from the grief of my loss I could not rejoice in their loss because I knew what that felt like when it happened to me.

If that company and I had practiced love in some of the areas I have mentioned above we would have positioned ourselves to win and perhaps they would have won my loyalty and that of the company that left them and if I had practiced love on them in the beginning perhaps they would have given me what was due me. What each of us would have gained would have been more lucrative than what we both eventually ended up with. Why, because love never fails.

Another characteristic of love is rejoicing when things are right and when truth triumphs. This one is not as difficult to remember but it is seldom done. Many times when we hear of something right and truthful that has happened to someone, unless it is a family member or a good friend and sometimes not even them we are non-responsive, complacent or just ignore the good news that we just heard. Our response is usually "that's nice" or "good for you". We do that because that person is going through their time of rejoicing, it is them and not us.

Love operates the same way all the time. We should be rejoicing for that person and with them. Now, the judgment of what is a celebration for one person but maybe not for the other person involved with this current victory.

What if you are on the other end of the judgment and what is right and truth is totally against what you did or what you represent. Love will still rejoice with you because love always operates the same way. Usually when that happens people are not so quick to rejoice.

I remember one time I ran a yellow light going to work and it is at an intersection that it seems as soon as you get near it turns yellow, I decided to speed up whenever I was approaching it so that I could get through faster. I did that so many times I cannot count them but one day I was seen by a policeman and I received a traffic ticket for a moving violation. Now the battle is on because I did not want that on my record because I knew that it would impact my car insurance rate and be counted as a point against my driver's license so I chose to go to court to fight it. I knew that I was wrong but I was hoping to get mercy from the judge.

During the time of my waiting I was thinking of all kind of things I could say to vindicate myself but none of them would be what was right and truth and during that process I decided that I would never make speeding up to make it through a yellow light a habit. That is what I needed to learn and when the trial came I knew that I had absolutely no way to defend myself so I prayed and asked God to help me and let me not have to say anything because I knew if the judge asked me anything I was going to lie and come up with some crazy story that was not right and not the truth. I really wanted to say what was right and truthful but I knew God heard my prayer and the way He did it baffled me at the time. I saw the officer there that was to testify against me and as the names were called on the docket I waited for my name to be called and what a long wait that was because my last name starts with a "W" and they started with the A's, by the time the s's were called the judge selected a group of people to go to another court room for their trials and my name was called to go. I left to go but the officer that was to testify against me did not come to the next court room. As a result when my name was called there was no one there to testify against me and I was released from the charge that I was guilty of.

I wanted to choose the characteristics of love that rejoice in what is right and truth and God honored that and vindicated me. That taught me a lesson that I will never forget and that is to own up to your stuff when it is not right and truth, practice what is right and truthful by admitting and quitting the other stuff. Now it is easy for me to rejoice in what is right and truth and it is also easy for me not to judge someone else that struggles with doing that.

Love wants to vindicate every one of us and cause us to win our battles but we can only enjoy that benefit if we embrace and rejoice in what is right and truth. What is right is right whether we do what is right or not and the truth will triumph whether we try to avoid it or not. Why? Because it is love and love never fails.

This next characteristic of love is more difficult because it requires us not to insist on our own rights or your own way, for love is not self-seeking; it is not touchy or fretful or resentful; it takes no account of the evil done to it nor does love pay any attention to a suffered wrong. This one is a series of actions that work together for the final result. This is one most people do not pay attention because almost everyone set themselves and what they want above everyone else. Hardly anyone can say that they are not sometimes touchy, fretful or resentful these seem to be the answer we come up when we experience a wrong that has been done to us. We more often than not want to get revenge and do take an account of the evil that has been done to us and we certainly pay close attention to all suffered wrong that we have to put up with. Our common reply is saying some kind of rebuttal in our defense or singing a "somebody done me wrong" song.

I heard an example of this that I was surprised to hear because I do not usually tell these kind of stories. Someone was telling me a lady gave her testimony on a radio station of how she used love to escape rape. Her report was that she was accosted by a person with a knife that forced her on the back seat and proceeded to try to rape her and she begin to tell him how much she love him as a person and he kept telling her to shut up or he was going to cut her into many pieces and her reply was and every piece of me will still love you. After he heard those words, he left the car and did not rape her. Why? Because love did not seek its own, it was touchy or fretful or resentful; it took no account of the evil being done to it at the time nor did love pay any attention to the suffered wrong of the attempted rape. The lady was freed from harm and let go and she won the battle by just practicing love. I was truly amazed, because who can think of loving someone that's committing a violent crime against you.

This of course is an extreme worse case and the majority of us will not be challenged with an opportunity like this one but what about your family members and friends, spouses and co-workers. How many opportunities do we have to not be self-seeking and just step back when we find ourselves in heated fellowship with someone? It may not be a person; it may be a company, an organization, a retail store or a laundry mat etc. That is one of the reason people like great customer service, because the entity providing the service is not self-seeking. We realize that their motivation is financial but many businesses do not practice loving customers in this area. They are self-seeking thinking they can refuse to love customers and get them to like it by mouth, word or deed. That customer will not sing their praises, nor will they be loyal, nor will they ever want to return. Well what about what we do! Our family, immediate or extended, friends and associates are our customers or any company that we want a favor from is also our customer. If we demonstrate bad customer service by not loving them with these characteristics of love we are going to get the same results as any company that gets low marks in customer service.

Another characteristic of love is the lack of fear which is found in 1 John 4:18.

1 John 4:18

There is no fear in love; but perfect love casteth out fear: because fear hath torment. He that feareth is not made perfect in love.

When you function in this characteristic you are not afraid of anything or anybody that comes along because there is no fear in love; in addition perfect love cast out fear because fear has torment. A person that does not fear is mature in love because they are able to tolerate anything and everything that shows up, and is ready to believe the best of every person, their hopes are fadeless under all circumstances and conditions, and they are able to withstand everything without wearying. For better understanding let us take a look at some of the Greek words in this passage. The word perfect in this passage is "teleios" which means of men full grown, adult, of full age, mature. The word torment is "kolasis" which means correction, punishment, penalty, this is important to understand because if you are mature in love you can cast out these things. The word cast is ballo which means to throw or let go of a thing without caring where it falls. In other words you let it go and do not care about the results.

If we know that God loves us and we do because He was willing to die for us, why do we not obey His word, I know what my reason was and that was fear that something bad that may happen to me if I did, in other words fear. You have to decide if that was your reason or not but the end result is that if we know that God loves us why do we fear anything that He tell us to do?

Why is love so important? Love never fails, everybody wants to be loved even those that say that they don't want love. Love is never turned down because it is an integral part of the need we have for each other. We have misunderstood the real essence of love because we have associated it primarily with the sexual love that we have for spouses, the family love we have for family members or the love we have for our friends and acquaintances. While all of these are real and necessary the true essence of love begins before any of these come into play.

To love anyone properly in any of the areas mentioned above we must understand the power of unconditional love. God is love and His love is unconditional. Nothing that is a part of God is ever going to fail, because He is God. Unconditional love is the kind of love that makes no excuses for not loving someone. Love is a decision that you make. It is not an automatic happening. Once you decide to love someone disregarding any condition or circumstance that they may find themselves in you are able to love them properly in any or all of the above areas of love. However, if you can make a decision to love someone you can also make a decision not to love someone. It has nothing to do with them; it is all about you and your decisions.

I have heard many songs and also some people stating concerning someone that they have a romantic interest (someone they may be considering for marriage) "I fell in love" with him or her or I am falling in love. Those are just statement describing their process of evaluating the person so that they can make a decision to love them or not.

It is very easy to love someone that loves you or treat you with some kind of kindness or at least do not make you angry, however those that disregard your person, disrespect and dishonor you or hate (means to love less) you are the ones that you will find it very difficult to love them. This is where making a decision to love people becomes very important because loving people unconditionally calls for a definite unshakable decision to do so. Once you make the decision to love unconditionally then you are ready for spousal, family and brotherly love. You can't love in any of these areas if you do not love the person unconditionally first.

I have heard people use respect as a substitute for love. Respect is not love. The definition of respect is a feeling of deep admiration for someone or something elicited by their abilities, qualities, or achievements or admires (someone or something) deeply, as a result of their abilities, qualities, or achievements. When people do this they have a serious problem staying in relationships that are established based on respect. The reason for that is the fact that as soon a person no longer have the ability, quality or achievement that is expected the decision to love them is changed to no longer loving them. For instance, if a woman marries a man because of his beautiful hair, that decision of loving him is going to change as soon as he starts the inevitable process of losing that hair because her love was based on respect not unconditional love. Respect is still needed but it is not unconditional love. If you disrespect anything it will disrespect you. For instance, if you do not respect your money by not giving it an assignment to pay a bill, to purchase grocery, to invest or whatever you need it to do it will get away from you and it will not take care of what you need it to do. Your money will be gone but none of the things that you needed it to do will be done, likewise if you disrespect people you are less likely to get the favor and grace from them that is available to anyone they decide to give it to.

Why is winning the battle so important? Because it works, that is one of the key components of what God did to bring mankind back into His presence, to free us from the penalty, the power and eventually the presence of sin. We see this in John 3:16.

John 3:16

For God so loved the world, that he gave his only begotten Son, that whosoever believeth in him should not perish, but have everlasting life.

We see from that God won the war, He loved us, and then He gave something very valuable and precious His only begotten son. Because God has won the war, we only have to fight the battles that confront us from time to time. God's motives are clear in this verse, and that is what we can expect when we fight battles with love, the same kind of victories. What is so amazing about this verse is that every believer that I have met knows it, even the children. What was the war that God had to win? God created man (Adam) as an object of His Love; through Christ, He created us to worship Him. This is something that we take for granted especially in the covenant that we have with God today, in this dispensation of grace. When Adam and the woman ate of the fruit of the tree that God told them not to eat of in an act of deliberate disobedience God did not get angry with them and wipe them from the face of the earth. Instead He operated in an act of love. Their sin caused them to be shifted from where they were a place of life to an unfamiliar place of dying, but that was not a time of meanness or rudeness to them, instead God set out to create an environment where man would eventually come into His presence and there would be no opportunity for that to be changed by any outside force.

That passage does not say for God so hated the world, it says that He loved the world and nothing can stop love from accomplishing its assignment. Since we know that God won the war loving us enough to give up His precious Son, why is it so difficult for us to unconditionally love those people that we see every day? Why is it so difficult to suffer long with people, why is it so difficult to forgive people and free them from that debt you think that they owe you. We want people to pay for sins they commit, but that is impossible because Jesus has already paid the price for sin for everybody. He paid the price for the world. We cannot make Him go to the cross again for our personal vendettas. Even if the person has wronged us Jesus has paid for that and that makes it easy for us to set them free. The price is right because that price is 0.

Chapter 9 – Love is Barometer for All Assignments

This subject is talked about a lot but we have a challenge sometimes because we have not considered a very important part of love being such an important part of our covenant with God. Love accompanies everything that we are commanded to do. All of God's covenants and dispensations are accompanied with love because God is love. He does nothing without love in mind. He has positioned us through Christ to never be without love, we just have to recognize what love is and what it is not. Some of us think that we can adhere to the principles, components, rules and regulations that the Lord has commanded us to do and get the results that theWord of God says that we would get without even thinking about whether or not you have attached love as a part of the process, however, you cannot do any of it without applying love to the formula. All of the characteristics of love that we talked about above apply but you have to apply it with wisdom.

It does not even matter what we think about in our mind we have to apply love because it is necessary for every part of our physical and practical life. It applies in our employment and things like that, I know at least three people that were having a challenge this year with people at their place of employment because they were not liked for whatever reason. They were attacked at every turn to the point where they were not sure if they were going to be able to keep their jobs, they all reported to me their acts of love toward those persons. They did not try to constantly defend themselves from criticism of their character, ability to do the work or their integrity and they did say that they were concerned about losing their jobs because of the attacks or the sabotage. These people were obvious enemies, but were not treated with what they were dishing out in like kind as the world teaches to be done. They were loved by the people that they attacked, eventually the attackers were the ones that lost their jobs and the ones being attacked remained on the job and received a raise as well. What happened? They all knew how to love their enemies and they practiced the Word of God found in Matthew 5:44.

Matthew 5:44

> *But I say unto you, Love your enemies, bless them that curse you, do good to them that hate you, and pray for them which despitefully use you, and persecute you;*

They were operating in love but they also had faith that they would not lose their jobs and that their work would speak for them no matter what their enemies were saying. Faith and Love worked together causing them to win the battle and get a raise. In this instance we have Love and Faith working together, love is what makes faith work, so we need to love before we apply faith. That is found in Galatians 5:6.

Galatians 5:6

For in Jesus Christ neither circumcision availeth any thing, nor uncircumcision; but <u>faith which worketh by love.</u>

This is one of the compliments that Paul gives to Philemon in Philemon 1:4-5.

Philemon 1:4-5

4 I thank my God, making mention of thee always in my prayers, 5 Hearing of thy love and faith, which thou hast toward the Lord Jesus, and toward all saints.

Paul even says to him that he mentions him always in his prayers. Paul said the same thing to the Ephesians in Ephesians 1:15-16 and to the Colossians in Colossians 1:3-4.

Ephesians 1:15-16

15 Wherefore I also, after I heard of your faith in the Lord Jesus, and love unto all the saints, 16 Cease not to give thanks for you, making mention of you in my prayers;

Colossians 1:3-4

> *3 We give thanks to God and the Father of our Lord Jesus Christ, praying always for you, 4 Since we heard of your faith in Christ Jesus, and of the love which ye have to all the saints,*

When we operate in love God sees that because God is love. Paul tells Timothy that faith and love is in Christ Jesus in 1Timothy 1:14.

> *1 Timothy 1:14*
>
> *And the grace of our Lord was exceeding abundant with faith and love which is in Christ Jesus.*

So we know that faith and love are partners because both are mentioned as being in Christ Jesus. Paul also pairs love with patience of hope and faith in 1 Thessalonians 1:3

> *1 Thessalonians 1:3*
>
> *Remembering without ceasing your work of faith, and labour of love, and patience of hope in our Lord Jesus Christ, in the sight of God and our Father;*

In order to get a good understanding let us take a look at a few of the other attributes that partner with love in Christ:

- Peace and Love – *2 Corinthians 13:11 Finally, brethren, farewell. Be perfect, be of good comfort, be*

of one mind, live in peace; and the God of love and
peace shall be with you.
- Love and Good Works - *Hebrews 10:24 And let us
consider one another to provoke unto love and to
good works:*

- Love and Honor - *Romans 12:10 Be kindly
affectioned one to another with brotherly love; in
honour preferring one another;*

- Love and Service - *Galatians 5:13 For, brethren, ye
have been called unto liberty; only use not liberty for
an occasion to the flesh, but by love serve one
another*

- Love and the Spirit of Meekness – *1 Corinthians 4:21
What will ye? shall I come unto you with a rod, or in
love, and in the spirit of meekness?*

- Edifying the Body and Love - *Ephesians 4:16 From
whom the whole body fitly joined together and
compacted by that which every joint supplieth,
according to the effectual working in the measure of
every part, maketh increase of the body unto the
edifying of itself in love.*

- Love and Offerings and Sacrifices - *Ephesians 5:2
And walk in love, as Christ also hath loved us, and
hath given himself for us an offering and a sacrifice
to God for a sweetsmelling savour.*

- Grace and Love - *Ephesians 6:24 Grace be with all them that love our Lord Jesus Christ in sincerity. Amen.*

- Love and Knowledge and All Judgment - *Philippians 1:9 And this I pray, that your love may abound yet more and more in knowledge and in all judgment;*

- Love in Deed and Truth – *1 John 3:18 My little children, let us not love in word, neither in tongue; but in deed and in truth.*

- Love and Rebuke - *Revelation 3:19 As many as I love, I rebuke and chasten: be zealous therefore, and repent.*

You cannot even speak the truth without doing it in love as seen in Ephesians 4:15.

Ephesians 4:15

But speaking the truth in love, may grow up into him in all things, which is the head, even Christ:

And when we speak the truth in love that will cause us to grow in all things in Christ. We cannot do anything without laboring in love, employing love or partnering with love. This just passes any understanding that we can logically think of, love is a part of who God is and it cannot be avoided in any area of our lives, therefore it is imperative that we make it a part of our lifestyle.We see that in Ephesians 3:19.

Ephesians 3:19
And to know the love of Christ, which passeth knowledge, that ye might be filled with all the fulness of God

The love of Christ goes pass any knowledge that we have and it is that love that causes us to be filled with all of the fullness of God. This is how God won the war of the law of God that was working against us because of sin as stated in Romans 13:10.

Romans 13:10

Love worketh no ill to his neighbour: therefore love is the fulfilling of the law.

Jesus did not get rid of the law, He fulfilled the law. There is noting that we can do or need to do to win the war of sin against us and God because Jesus has done all that is required. God loved us all, in fact He loved everything, He loved the world.

Jesus said that people will know His disciples by the love they have for one another.

John 13:35

By this shall all men know that ye are my disciples, if ye have love one to another.

Not by the signs, wonders and miracles, even though believers are able to do that but this is not how they shall know that we are Jesus' disciples, they will know only by the love we have for one another. John reminds us that no man has seen God, but if we love one another His love will be seen in our lives and that love of His is perfected in us.

1 John 4:12

No man hath seen God at any time. If we love one another, God dwelleth in us, and his love is perfected in us.

If you do not have a lifestyle of love working in your life already, today is a good day to start. You will never be disappointed if you do, things won't change but your response to them will change. You will experience a peace that you cannot explain to people and you will never fear being loved again because when you do this you realized that God loves you and the reason you love people has nothing to do with them, they did nothing to cause you to love them and they can do nothing to stop it, what freedom that will bring to your life.

One of the greatest things that we can do for someone is to love them deeply and also one of the greatest things that can happen to you and I is for someone to love us deeply. This is very important because even though we are free from the penalty of sin, the power of sin and eventually the presence of sin we still sin. As believers we are not sinners but we do sin. That is one of the things that we can be sure that Satan will do and that is to be an accuser of the brethren. Accusing believers day and night so that he can go to God and get permission to take advantage of us, but if we love deeply we can cover the person and stop Satan in his tracks. We find this in 1 Peter 4:8.

1 Peter 4:8

Above all; love each other deeply, because love covers over a multitude of sins.

The amplified version of 1 Peter 4:8 says it this way:

Above all things have intense and unfailing love for one another, for love covers a multitude of sins [forgives and [e]disregards the offenses of others].

When we love people to the degree that we disregard any offense that they do to us, we cover them from the tricks and the wiles of Satan, because we love we cover them. God is love and when He sees that we are covering them He covers them. They do not have to take a beating from Satan. I remember one time I had a vision about myself, I had done something wrong, I can't remember what I did but I do remember that I did it. And there were people there trying to get me to admit it. I did not want to do it at first, but I finally I said I know I am wrong and I said OK and then I picked up a 2 x 4 and gave it to them to hit me with. I thought that they were just going to beat me for doing what I did, but the person that got the opportunity to swing the 2 x 4 was Satan. He took it and hit me in the back of my head and tried to kill me. The blow was so hard I thought that I should have died but I did not. It did however; knock my right eye out of its socket. I knew that I could recover because I did not die but I was not expecting a blow that hard. I took a class called the Revelations of God from Bishop R. S. Walker's Ministries School of Prophets that focused on dreams, visions, trances and other revelations of God and it helped me with the understanding. I already knew what had happened and why but what I did not understand until just this moment was that the people that were accusing me could have covered me and freed me from that accusations. They could have forgiven me and disregarded the offense. But they did not, then I understood, how many times that I had done that to someone. As I begin to ponder what I had done so many time to family and friend by giving Satan the opportunity to do what he does to people when there is no love covering them because of unforgiveness and lack of intense love.

Peter was talking to believers, people like you and I if you are saved. He wanted us to understand how much God loved that person that did that offense to us and to love them intensely by forgiving them and covering their sin. God wants us to tap into His very nature and for love to be shown in deed not just in words, love is not driven by emotions it is a conscious decision to obey the word of God that makes love a lifestyle.

This same thing applies to sinners. We find that in James 5:20.

James 5:20

> ***Let him know, that he which converteth the sinner from the error of his way shall save a soul from death, and shall hide a multitude of sins***

It may be possible for some people to want Satan to kill people but I do not think that most of us do. I know that I don't.

Paul explains this better in 2 Corinthians 2:10-11.

> ***2 Corinthians 2:10-11***
>
> ***10 To whom ye forgive any thing, I forgive also: for if I forgave any thing, to whom I forgave it, for your sakes forgave I it in the person of Christ; 11 Lest Satan should get an advantage of us: for we are not ignorant of his devices.***

The Amplified version of 2 Corinthians 2:10-11 says:

> ***If you forgive anyone anything, I too forgive that one; and what I have forgiven, if I have forgiven anything, has been for your sakes in the presence [and with the approval] of Christ (the Messiah), To keep Satan from getting the advantage over us; for we are not ignorant of his wiles and intentions.***

Now that I have a better understanding of this I purpose to forgive quickly and to love more than I have ever done before. I don't know of a person on the planet that I do not love but needless to say I will never meet all of the people on the planet so I speak that by faith because there is no distance in the spirit. It is much easier to love people that hate you from a distance or even people who for whatever reason just don't like you and you know it than it is to love those that deliberately hurt you. That is a true test of love because the only ones that get an opportunity to do that are the ones that are very close to you. Perhaps that is because those are the ones you least expect and when they do it sometimes it is a total shock. However, you still have to love them deeply and do not take any account of the wrong that was done to you. This means that they will get an opportunity to do it again because you have to love them as if they never did anything at all to you.

When you take the time to think about love from the surface it may seem hard to do but if you remember that God does all of the work then it is easy. It is not possible to love like God does without God because He is the source and we need the help of the Holy Spirit to make that happen. Dr. James Orr, General Editor of the International Standard Bible Encyclopedia Original 1915 Edition puts it all in perspective, he said "Christianity is the only religion that sets forth the Supreme Being as Love. In heathen religions He is set forth as an angry being and in constant need of appeasing." I have seen some photos and statutes of their gods and they look fighting as meant to instill fear, but there is no fear in perfect love. God has already set the stage for our victory because He has won the war and He has given us a battle plan. All we have to do is employ love to win every battle, we do have to fight but the fight is fixed and we win. Sin is the reason for fights and we know from Proverbs 10:12.

About The Author

Dr. Cynthia V. White graduated from Ballard Hudson High School in Macon, Georgia. She continued her education at Morris Brown College, Atlanta, Georgia where she received a Bachelor of Science Degree in Mathematics and Education. She has also received a Master of Arts in Biblical Studies, Master of Divinity and a Doctor of Ministry from Maple Springs Baptist Bible College and Seminary, Capitol Heights, Maryland.

Cynthia was employed by the Department of the Navy for 31 years. During her tenure there, she was the head of the following departments: Computer Aided Design and Manufacturing, Industrial Improvement Technologies, Joint Electronic Drawings and Manufacturing of Industrial Data, Military Construction Projects, Service Craft Management and Manufacturing Technology Program Manager for Naval Shipyards. Cynthia is an accomplished conference speaker. She has spoken at the national productivity conferences, naval engineering conferences, research conferences, production conferences and general business conferences.

Cynthia is a strong supporter of community services. She has participated in fund raisers for the March of Dimes and she supports children in need programs. She has been the Chairman of the Board of Directors of the Center for Community Development of Housing for the Mentally Ill and the Aged. She has also been member of the Board of Directors of Bethel House, a community support center for people in need of help and assistance food, housing, education, jobs and other needs.

Currently is a member of Heritage Church International, Waldorf, Maryland where Bishop Rodney S. Walker I serves as Senior Pastor. Under Bishop Walker's leadership and covering, Cynthia serves as the Secretary of Records of the church, Office Manager. She has also served as manager of Kingdom Christian Bookstore. She serves on the staff of Heritage Church International as a Chief Elder, the Overseer of the Apostolic Arm of the ministry and as an Associate Pastor. She has ministered as conference speaker for women, prophetic conferences, financial and business conferences and workshops. She has taught Bible Study at the Department of the Navy under the directions of the Chaplain for the Naval Sea System Command.

Cynthia serves in Bishop R. S. Walker Ministries, where Bishop R. S. Walker is founder and President, as Registrar and head the Registration Department of the School of Prophets and as a Prophetic Presbyter of the ministry. She is an instructor in the Bishop R.S. Walker Ministries Bible College.

Cynthia is the owner and the CEO of her own business. She is accomplished author. She has published three books, Understanding Spiritual Maturity, The Christian Torah and What Your Father Never Told You about Business. She has spoken at several conferences on the subjects of the books. She is preparing to publish the following books: The Power of Seed, The Sycamore Fig Tree – A Living Sacrifice and the Power of the Earth.

www.ingramcontent.com/pod-product-compliance
Lightning Source LLC
Chambersburg PA
CBHW071132090426
42736CB00012B/2098